Flying Colors

Design Quilts with Freeform Shapes & Flying Geese

GAIL GARBER

C&T PUBLISHING

Publisher: Amy Marson

Creative Director: Gailen Runge

Acquisitions Editor: Susanne Woods

Editor: Liz Aneloski

Technical Editors: Sandy Peterson and Janice Wray

Copyeditor/Proofreader: Wordfirm Inc.

Cover Designer: Kristen Yenche

Book Designer: Kristy Zacharias

Production Coordinator: Zinnia Heinzmann

Production Editor: Alice Mace Nakanishi

Illustrator: Tim Manibusan

Photography by Christina Carty-Francis and Diane Pedersen of C&T Publishing, Inc., unless otherwise noted

Published by C&T Publishing, Inc., P.O. Box 1456, Lafayette, CA 94549

Library of Congress Cataloging-in-Publication Data

Garber, Gail.

Flying colors : design quilts with freeform shapes & flying geese : 5 paper-pieced projects, full-size foundations / by Gail Garber.

p. cm.

ISBN 978-1-57120-818-7 (soft cover)

1. Patchwork--Patterns. 2. Quilting. I. Title.

TT835.G33165 2010

746.46'041--dc22

2009051480

Printed in China

10 9 8 7 6 5

Contents

Dedication

To my students:

Their work inspires me with its creativity and originality. It is from them that I continue to learn new, improved methods and techniques to add to my repertoire, as well as gain an ever-increasing community of quilting friends.

Acknowledgments

I thank Donna Barnitz, my incredible assistant and friend of twenty years. Many of the quilts in this book were a collaboration of our team of two. In addition to patiently editing and formatting text and critiquing designs, color choices, and fabrics, sometimes vociferously, Donna makes the quilts sing with her beautiful and creative machine quilting. I appreciate her honesty when she lets me know in no uncertain terms that my choices for a particular design are less than wonderful or otherwise not to her liking. Our working style—that of longtime friends unafraid to disagree—is the best possible environment to inspire creativity.

My quilting group of fifteen years, Designing Women, is an integral part of this book, and many of the members' quilts appear on the pages of this book: Mary Chappelle, Cathy Combs, Patricia Drennan, Michele Hymel, Anita McSorley, and Lisa Stewart. Through our monthly meetings, we continued to explore new designs and techniques that became the body of work for this book.

If it weren't for Ann Silva, of Ann Silva's Bernina Sewing Center in Albuquerque, New Mexico, I may not have followed this creative path. It was Ann who strongly encouraged my early teaching efforts and introduced me to the wonderful world of Bernina. I also thank Bernina of America for the ongoing support and for including me in the Bernina Artisans program.

I thank my editor, Liz Aneloski, for her patience and guidance through this process, and C&T Publishing for having confidence in this book.

Finally, I thank my daughter, Christi Garber, and my sister, Ann Rhodes, who believe in me and encourage me to always strive for greater heights. I love you.

Preface

When circumstances plunked me down smack-dab in the middle of New Mexico in 1973, I had little idea of the wonders that were to come. My home state, the Land of Enchantment, is just that—a magical place: 121,593 forgotten square miles between Texas and Arizona; sense of humor required for occupancy. Our nation's fifth largest state boasts officially designated specialties: turquoise, the bolo tie, the roadrunner, the chile, and the *bizcochito,* our state cookie! It is simply enchanting, from the grandeur of the landscape to the peculiar antics of the folks that call it home. Quirkiness counts here; differences are celebrated and not constrained. It was here, surrounded by the unconventional, that quilting called my name.

I learned to quilt in 1980. Our fabrics were calicoes in pale hues, with white, off-white, beige, or muslin backgrounds. There were "rules" too: a quilt wasn't authentic unless hand stitched, yellow would kill a quilt, and the backing should show off your beautiful stitches. But my stitches weren't so lovely. I tried to join a quilting bee, but the ladies didn't like the way this left-handed novice plied the fabric with her needle. Maybe it was an act of kindness, although it smarted at the time. As I look back now, almost 30 years later, I marvel that quilting held such a strong appeal, one that still has me firmly enthralled.

Those early quilts were the foundation for assimilating techniques learned from many classes over the years. I loved art quilts and was inspired by Katie Pasquini's work. In her mandala class, while experimenting with free-form design, I learned to make fearless color choices. Although I didn't know it then, I was improving the skills that would become an invaluable part of my quilter's toolbox.

Big Bang by Gail Garber, 1997, 70″ × 78″

In 1997, I made my epiphany quilt, *Big Bang*. In this quilt, I was finally able to integrate the skills learned over seventeen years. It also represents the first time I successfully wove the three basic elements of a quilt top—foreground, background, and borders—into one homogeneous design. The foreground boldly asserts its prominence, while the background provides subtle motion and the border blinks in and out. I've never looked at a design with the same eyes since then.

One of my greatest joys is helping students discover the designers within themselves and learn that they really can create original designs. One of the added benefits of teaching is learning from my students. One student wanted a porthole-like fish border to frame a round underwater scene. We figured out how to make fish. Another asked, "How do I make a tree?" So the story goes—teaching and learning, learning and teaching.

This book builds on my quilting and life experience and that of my students. I hope you find inspiration within these pages and the courage to try the unknown.

—*Gail*

Inspiration and Learning

Each of us is influenced by our surroundings and the things we see in our everyday life, such as the landscape and colors of the neighborhood, nature, weather, the change of the seasons, and even the unexpected.

One of my quilts, *Dawn of the New Day* (on the right), was inspired by a national tragedy, 9/11, which I chose to interpret in an abstract way. When I made this quilt for the invitational United We Quilt exhibit, memorializing the events of that terrible day in American history, I knew I did not want a visual image of the World Trade Center. Instead, I chose to represent it in a more figurative way. The somber gray flying geese show the rubble that remained, and the bright yellow "pointy dudes" represent the individual good deeds that happened as a result. It culminates in a bright, shining star of freedom, surrounded by the patriotism of America. It features a 10,000 pyramids border, a free-form star, pointy dudes, and flying geese.

Dawn of the New Day by Gail Garber, 2002, 48″ × 41″

Monarchs in Winter by Gail Garber and Donna Barnitz, 2009, 14″ × 16½″

We visit other countries and learn from their cultures, perhaps not in person, but through the pages of a magazine or the Internet. Although I've never visited the wintering grounds of the Monarch butterfly, I was inspired by a cover of *National Wildlife* magazine that showed the beautiful butterflies resting on vegetation.

Land of the Midnight Sun by Gail Garber, Michele Hymel, and Donna Barnitz, 2009, 31″ × 26″

I recently returned from a teaching trip to Anchorage, Alaska, where the sun didn't set until after 11 p.m. daily and had already risen by the time I awoke each morning. They call it the Land of the Midnight Sun. Although the summer is drenched in nearly 24-hour sunshine, the winter months are dark. It is then that the light emanates from another source, the aurora borealis, which I have never seen. However, I found a wonderful piece of "aurora" fabric in Sylvia's Quilt Depot in Wasilla, Alaska. It was the inspiration for this collage of all things northern: the aurora, the black spruce, the brilliant sun, and the lengthened nights of winter. I began the drawing in class, as a teaching exercise, and continued to work on it when I returned home—a lasting memory of a trip to a beautiful state.

Our friends influence our perception of the world and how we interpret it through art and our quilts. Fabric use also might be influenced by the way our local quilt shop makes purchases. Color use and texture can vary widely among regions, and sometimes even within the same community. Quiltmakers in some areas fill their quilts with a riot of colors, while the quilts from other areas feature more serene hues and prints and more subtle designs. Still others prefer the rich earth-toned colors that are often referred to as "country."

I am fortunate to work closely with a small group of quilting friends, some of whom I have known for twenty years and most for over ten. We call ourselves Designing Women. The group functions as a critique group, a support group, and sometimes just an eating group. We meet monthly, more or less, depending on what we are working on at that particular time. We have become fast friends with an easy patter to our meetings, gently poking fun and helping with well-intentioned suggestions. Of course, the final decision always belongs to the maker of the quilt. Over the years, we have participated in several challenges, made community-service raffle quilts, and, during one year, completed a round-robin quilt. This small group is my quilting network, friends whom I trust to express their honest opinions, as well as willing testers for new ideas. I find solace in this group.

Joining my local quilting group back in 1983 was instrumental in my quilting education as well as my personal growth. Learning to feel comfortable in the large group and speaking on a stage and into a microphone was a huge challenge to overcome for this formerly shy individual. I learned that the world is not such a frightening place but is full of potential friends, people who share my passions and are just itching to help me learn new skills and to learn from me.

Sometimes I hear stories from solo quilters, those lacking a support group of any kind. They may be new to the community, shy, or unaware that a local quilting group exists. Whenever possible, extend a gentle hand of friendship to each new quilter that you meet. Let her know about local quilt groups, shops, and upcoming quilt shows. Some of my best friends around the globe connected via the worldwide sisterhood of quilters. One of the best learning experiences of my life was working in a local quilt shop. In order to help customers, I had to learn to quickly help quilters select fabrics for their projects. I soon learned to enjoy working with colors formerly foreign to my palette. Unfortunately, working in the quilt shop was not a good economic decision for me. I was unable to resist all that temptation, and the month that I took home a ten-dollar paycheck, after working many hours, was my last. Still, it greatly expanded my horizons and appreciation for a wide array of fabrics, some of which have now become favorites.

Digital cameras and the associated photographic software have revolutionized our ability to record memories as well as to capture our surroundings. I almost always carry a small point-and-shoot camera with me so that I can take photos of anything that might be inspirational. Since there is no need to pay for film developing nowadays, it doesn't matter how many photos you take, or even if only one of dozens turns out to be a great shot. The delete button will take care of the rest. I set the screen saver on my monitor to play a random assortment of photos. Some of these become elements of quilt designs later.

Sometimes inspiration comes from within, as different events shape our lives. The result might be an abstract design with special meaning known only to the maker. Or, it may be completely geometric with graphic use of color. Sometimes, when I sit down with a blank piece of paper, I don't have any ideas. No conscious inspiration. Nothing! So, I draw one curved line and then add another. I keep on building on this. Sometimes it turns into something wonderful and sometimes it does not, but it gets me going.

Dare to draw without commitment, knowing that there is no obligation to stitch today's design. Some designers carry a small sketchbook to capture inspiration as it occurs. Each time you work on a drawing, you are exercising your brain, strengthening the synapses, so later you'll have improved skills, a better sense of proportion, and greater confidence in your ability.

My Favorite Tools

Just a handful of the right tools can make your life so much easier. Designing and drawing require a few special tools that help you to be more successful and make the drawing process much simpler.

A **flexible curve** is an invaluable drawing tool. It enables you to bend the curve to audition lines and decide which will be best for your design. I prefer a flexible curve that is 32–40 inches long or more, because it will be more likely to reach from the beginning to the end of a line to be drawn. It is sometimes hard to position two smaller curves to achieve a seamless curve without a bump where they are placed end to end. Flexible curves are available from many quilt shops and arts and crafts shops; however, they are not all created equal. Look for a curve that bends fluidly without resistance. The curve does not need to have measurements already marked on it.

A good **drawing compass** that locks in place and has an extender bar is a sound investment. I prefer the Alvin 975VK compass that allows you to draw a circle up to 24 inches in diameter (Resources, page 79). It has quick-release tabs so you can easily change the size of the circle, as well as a fine-tuning dial for detail work. It includes a pencil holder, so you can use a mechanical pencil.

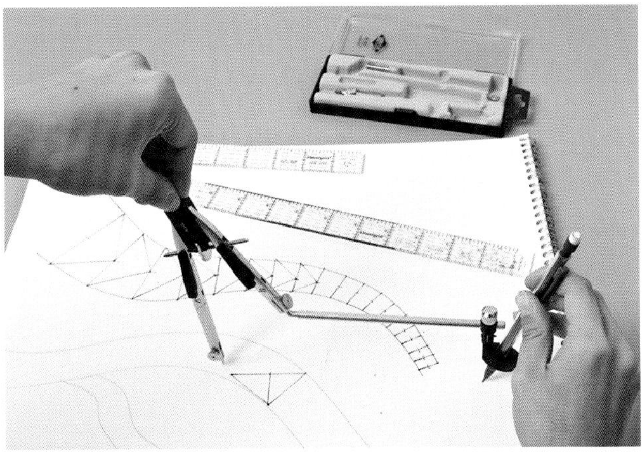

The **mechanical pencil** I prefer to use is the super-inexpensive BIC Clic with a 0.5mm lead. The clicker that advances the lead is on the end of the pencil where it will not interfere with drawing when placed inside the compass. And it has a good eraser. With its sturdier lead, it does not break as easily as some of the other pencils.

My favorite eraser is an **eraser pen** that looks like a mechanical pencil but holds an eraser instead. This nifty eraser can be refilled when needed, and its small diameter enables fine-detail erasing.

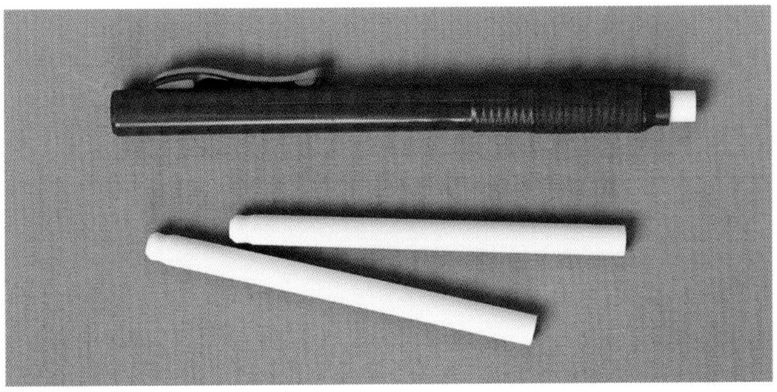

A **rotary cutting mat** under your drawing paper will hold it securely in place, and the point of the compass will stick into the mat during drawing, ensuring no slippage.

I use a variety of **rotary cutting rulers.** The 4-inch square rotary cutting ruler is absolutely the very best ruler for trimming curved shapes (see page 51 and Resources, page 79). The 1″ × 6″ or 1″ × 12″ rotary cutting rulers are the perfect size for filling in drawing details. They are the right size to hold in your hand and move easily on the paper.

An **Add-A-Quarter ruler** is a cool tool that works well to help trim seam allowances when paper-foundation piecing.

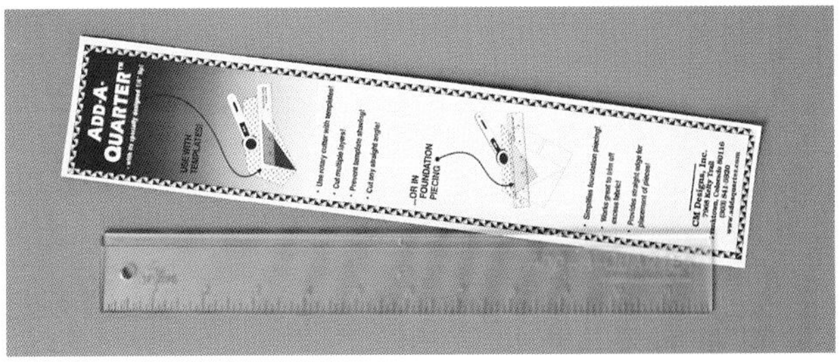

I use a **ceramic pencil marker** to transfer the registration marks to dark fabrics. Although it looks and feels like a mechanical pencil, it holds ceramic "leads" in a variety of refillable colors, so there is always the perfect color to show up on a fabric.

Freezer paper comes in rolls 12″, 15″, 18″, and 24″ wide; small 8½″ × 11″ sheets, and large 42″ × 42″ sheets (see Resources, page 79, for information on sheets). It works wonderfully for my paper-piecing technique.

That Purple Thang is a cute, very purple tool that looks like a cuticle pusher and is perfect to help remove paper foundations from the back of your project or for getting those obstinate tiny pieces that seem impossible to remove (Resources, page 79).

Designing with Free-Form Shapes

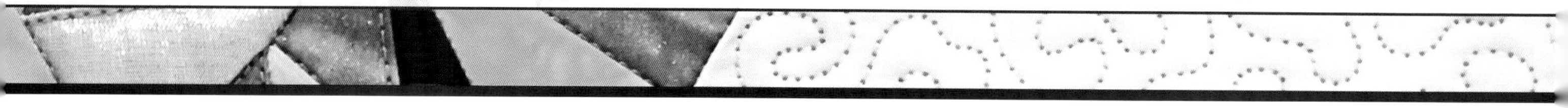

All elements in this type of quilt design are drawn as one homogeneous piece of work.

There is a central focus, as well as a background and borders, and they work together as a team. No one element stands alone. I believe that this makes for a more intriguing quilt design. The borders in my quilts come and go, disappearing behind a central design element and then reappearing. Similarly, the central design sometimes extends over the top of a border, while at other times, it disappears behind a border.

Take your time while designing. If and when you get stuck and cannot think of what to do next, take a break, maybe for several days. Although you will not be actively working on the design, your subconscious continues puzzling over what to do, especially while you are sleeping. Sometimes I wake up in the morning with the perfect solution.

Another suggestion is to work on several drawings or sketches before deciding on the final design. I keep all of these designs in a big drawer in my studio. While most of these will never become a completed quilt, there are elements in each that could be useful. Often, I return to this stash of drawings and review the languishing designs. I will notice the particular way a curve accented a design, or see a filler that is quite nice. Then, although the whole drawing might not appear in a quilt, the best part of it does

The number one suggestion for designing with free-form shapes is: *Big is easier to stitch than small!* One of your most valuable tools is the local photocopy shop, where your original drawing can be enlarged.

It is usually easier to visualize a design in progress when you can easily see the entire design on the table in front of you in a smaller size. Drawing in this smaller scale, you can draw proportionally appropriate elements that work cohesively in a design. The individual shapes at this scale, however, can be too small to easily stitch and may lack the emphasis necessary for a dramatic effect. So, draw in a small scale, perfect your design, and enlarge later. The photocopy shop is your friend. The following exercises will help you practice designing with free-form shapes.

The Goose Is Loose

Begin by creating a simple design on an 8½″ × 11″ sheet of paper. We will use the flexible curve and a ruler for this design.

Note

With the type of foundation piecing I recommend, the finished quilt top will be a mirror image of the final design drawn on the paper. *See the finished quilt on page 15.*

1. Use a flexible curve to draw 2 curved lines that are close together on one end, gracefully widening toward the lower right side. Can you see how this gives the drawing the illusion of distance? Graceful curves enhance the fluidity of these designs. Think big, flowing curves when drafting these types of designs. Think of this shape as the "yellow brick road."

Note

Don't draw the lines too close together or the geese will be too small to be easily pieced.

2. Round the corner of the goose strip. Suddenly, the design takes on a completely new perspective. Now there is a graceful, swooping curve, along with a curved edge that enhances the design.

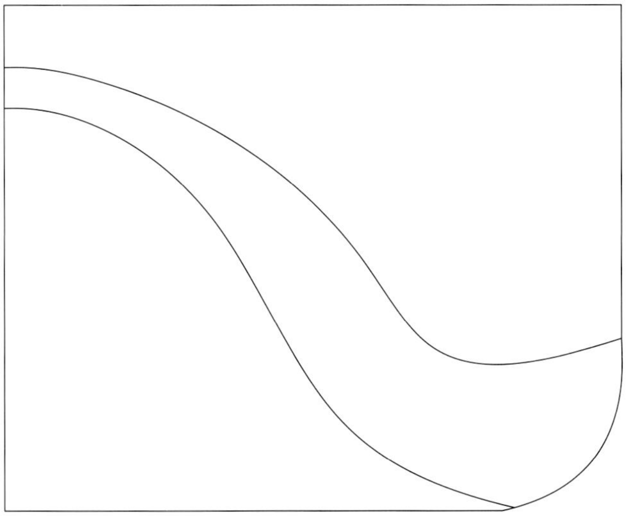

Draw curved lines, widening toward one side. Then, round a corner.

3. Fill in the "yellow brick road" with flying geese (page 21). When I draw this particular figure, I like to have the tip of the largest goose touch the outer edge.

4. Use your flexible curve to gently curve the bottom edge of the design. Also add a gently curved border to the bottom and the side. Now the overall design is taking shape and the negative space is receding. At this point in the design, the border could be simply a complementary fabric that enhances the rest of the quilt.

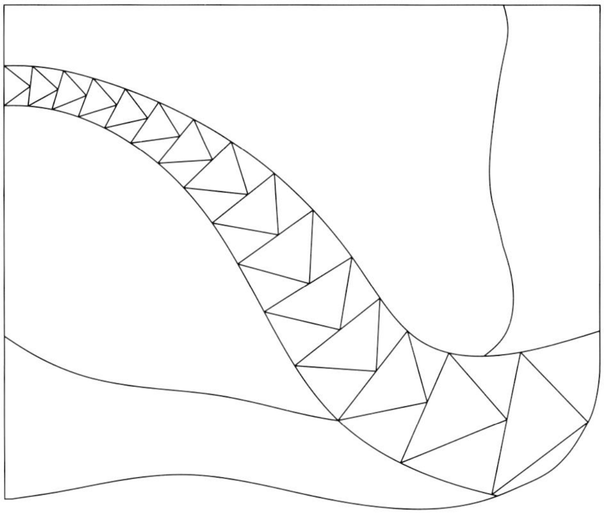

Fill in flying geese. Then, make bottom edge curvy and add curved bottom and side borders.

Effective designs often include more than one of a particular element. Let's add another row of geese, right next to the first row.

5. Use your flexible curve to add another line above the first row of geese. This time, stop drawing that line when it reaches the border.

6. Fill in with flying geese, but make sure when you are drawing the brickwork (pages 20–21) that these lines do not match the lines in the original set of flying geese. This eliminates the need to match every seam. If 1 line happens to match, that is okay. Now you have created 2 potential rows of geese, 1 that extends over the border and another that disappears behind the border. The design is becoming more complex.

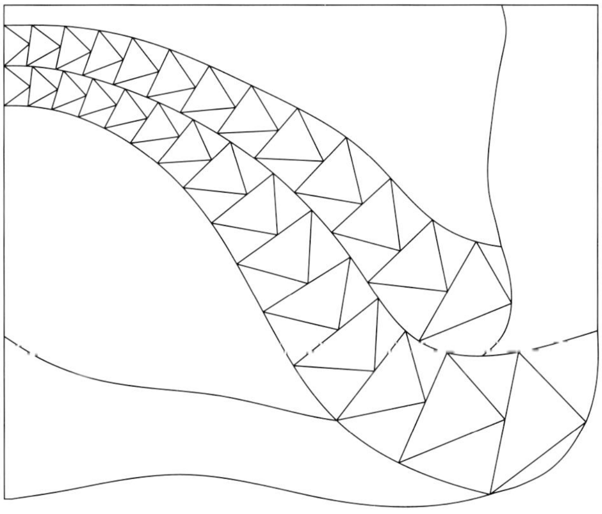

Draw another curvy line and add flying geese.

ADDING POINTY DUDES TO YOUR DESIGN

Pointy dudes (page 29) are a wonderful way to accent a design. To make them, further subdivide a goose (or 2) in the flying geese strip. They can be incorporated into a long row of geese, or they can be turned on their side to form a border. If made with an accent fabric that contrasts with the other fabrics, the dudes create an arrow effect and can be used to direct the viewer's eye toward a particular design element. They also can enhance the flow of a row of geese by adding a strong directional emphasis to a design.

Generally, I use only a sprinkling of pointy dudes in a design. Look for 2 or possibly 3 flying geese that are medium to large in size. The width of the dude is entirely arbitrary, but it should be wide enough so the contrasting fabric of the dude will show up against the other fabrics. I often find that bright yellow, lime green, or fuchsia make effective dudes. At other times, I include a whole row of pointy dudes in a border.

1. Draw 2 pointy dudes among the geese. Note that both are positioned in the lower right-hand corner where the geese are larger, and that I avoided the smaller, more distant geese.

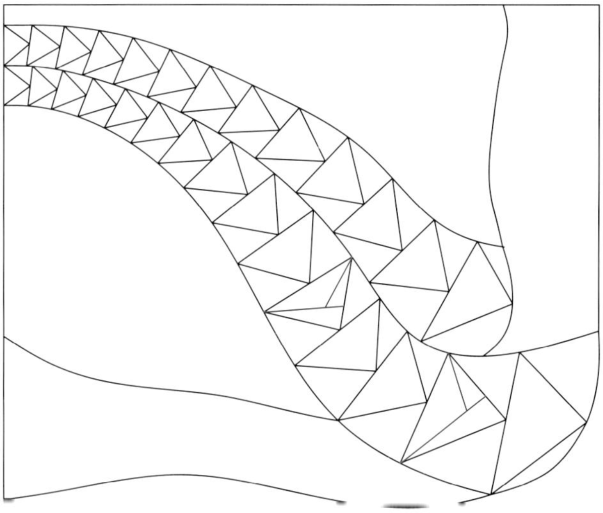

Add pointy dudes.

2. Draw the brickwork for the pointy dudes (page 20) in the border. Fill in even those areas that are partially covered by the flying geese row (green lines).

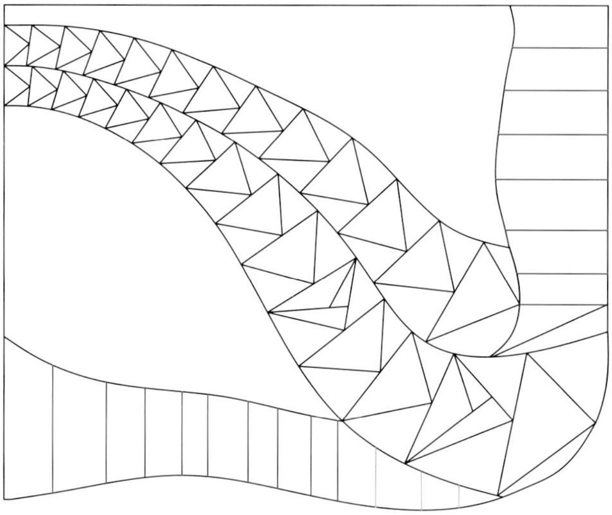

Add brickwork.

3. Add the first lines of the pointy dudes (red lines), including those that disappear behind the goose filler strip (green lines).

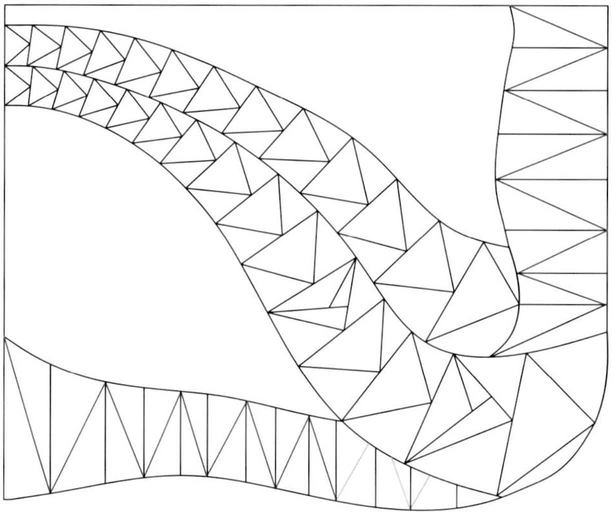

Draw first lines of pointy dudes.

4. Finish drawing the pointy dudes and erase the brick-work lines.

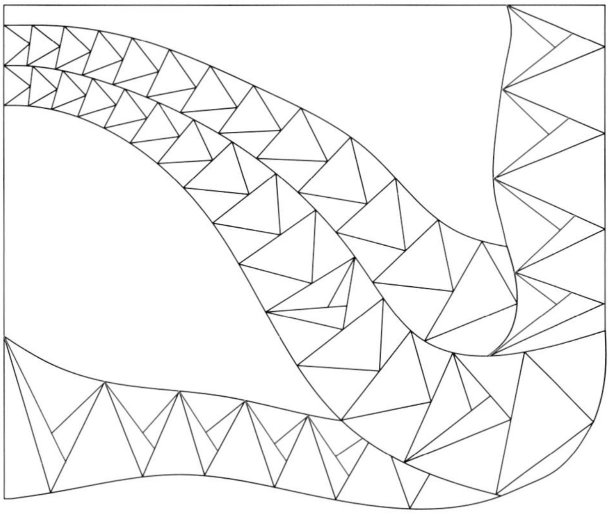

Finish drawing pointy dudes; erase unnecessary lines.

Completed project; mirror image of your final design drawing

Landscape Shapes

Now that you have mastered a couple of basic shapes, let's investigate shapes that form a landscape, such as tiny trees, rolling hills, and a sunrise/sunset. We will use a compass, a flexible curve, and a ruler for this rectangular design. We will finish this design by adding a 10,000 pyramids border and a row of pointy dudes across the top.

TINY TREES DESIGN

1. Use a larger sheet of paper for this design, perhaps a piece of freezer paper that is wider than it is tall. Mark an X to indicate the center of a circle. Although you may not need to know where the center of the circle is located, it is always a good idea to mark the center, just in case it becomes necessary to find it later. Then, draw a circle around the center X using a compass.

2. Draw a second X near the first. Close the compass a little, and draw a slightly smaller circle around this new center. Notice how the circles are offset, giving the illusion of a halo.

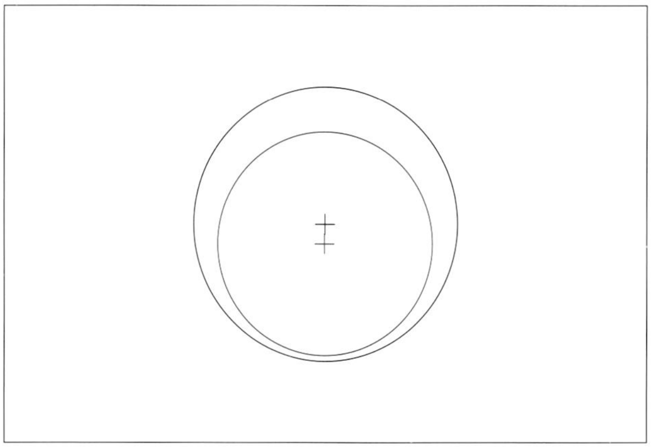

Draw 2 circles.

3. Add a rectangle outside the circles to enclose the design and provide boundaries within which to work.

If the design grows beyond these boundary lines, they can later be erased. However, setting boundaries can be helpful in determining the proportions of the free-form shapes within the design.

4. Use a flexible curve and draw 2 gracefully curving lines that will be filled with a design later.

tip

I find it helpful to draw all of the filler strips and shapes before filling them with the textures shown in the fillers chapter (pages 20–33).

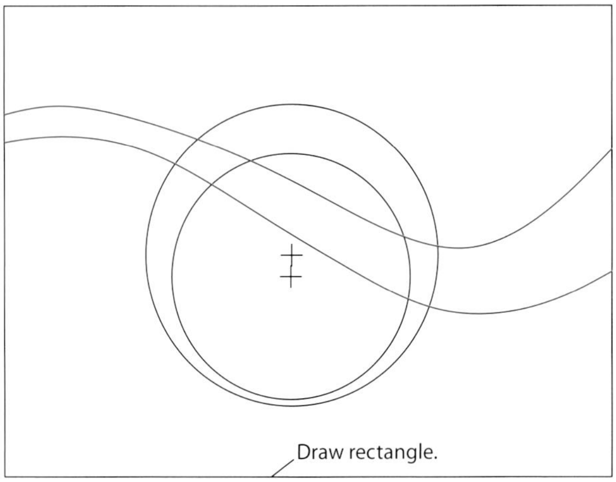

Draw rectangle around circles. Draw 2 curving lines.

5. Erase portions of the lines to create the illusion that the filler strip weaves through the offset halo.

Notice that I erased the narrower portion of the offset halo, thus eliminating a more difficult section to stitch.

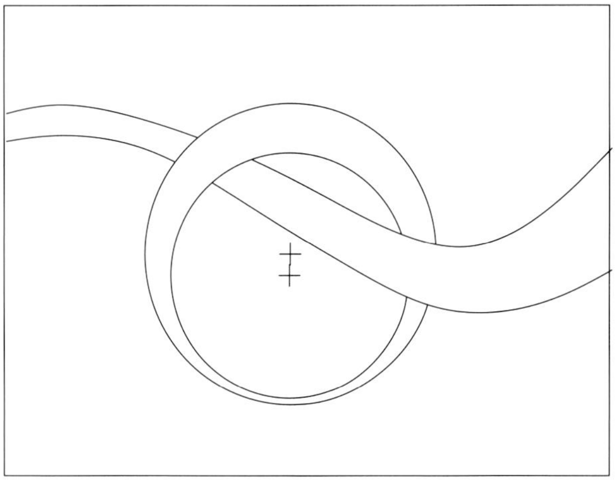

Erase some lines.

6. Draw another curved filler strip.

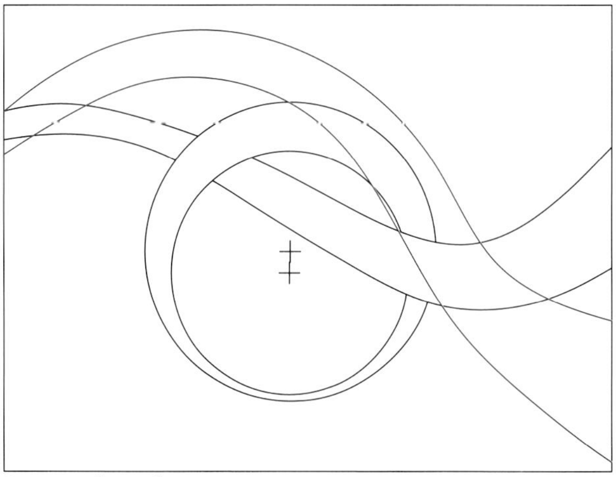

Draw another strip.

7. Erase portions of the filler strip, so it appears to weave in and out with the existing filler strip, as well as the offset halo.

I opted to make it appear as if the new filler strip partially disappears behind the halo. Notice that while the right side of the design looks balanced, the left side contains a fair amount of negative space in which there is nothing to hold the viewer's interest, essentially a void in the design. A strong design will be balanced with an equal proportion of elements in all sectors.

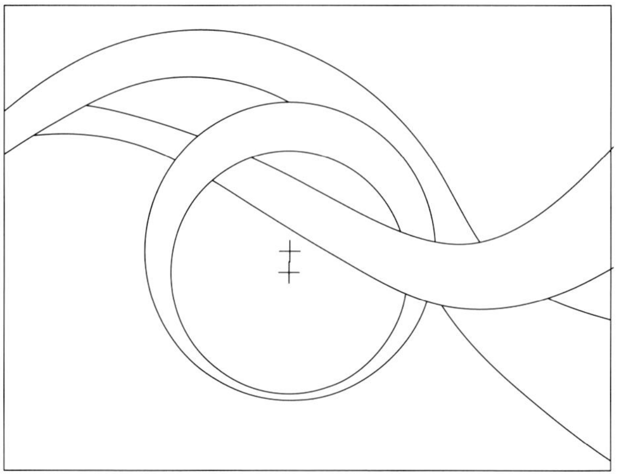

Erase some lines.

Let's work on the outer edges and bring them in closer to center the focus of the design so that it is more balanced. There is always the option to use straight edges, but sometimes a curved edge adds more interest.

8. Use a flexible curve to audition and draw the curved edges along the outer edges of the design.

9. If you like the way the curved edge looks, erase the straight lines.

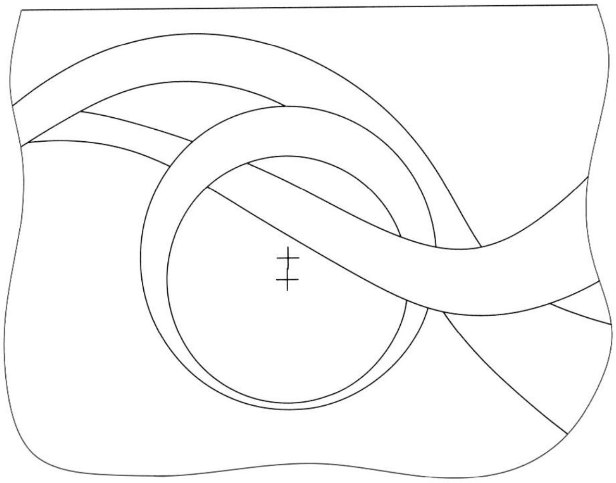

Draw curved edges and erase boundary lines.

> **tip**
>
> *It is always a good idea to use either a straight edge or a very gentle, almost flat curve on the top edge of the design. This will make it easier to hang your quilt.*

10. Add a straight-line border at the top of the design and erase the portion of the line that crosses over the top filler strip, making it appear that the filler strip is on top of the border.

11. Add a curved border to the remaining sides of the design. Decide which element you prefer to be on the top and erase the appropriate lines.

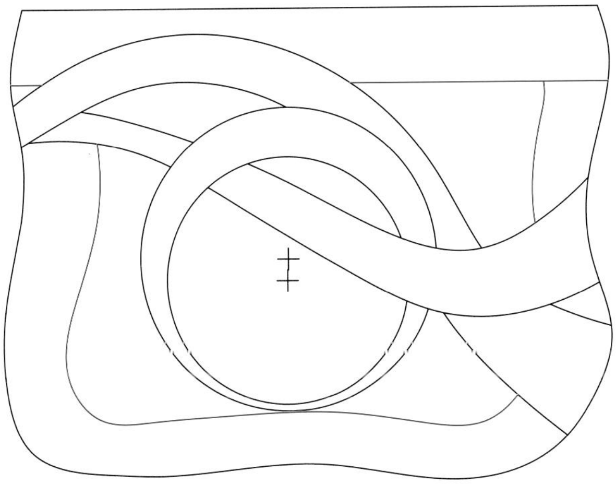

Draw top border line and erase unnecessary lines. Then, draw curved border lines and erase unnecessary lines.

12. Use the flexible curve to audition several lines that create the illusion of rolling hills along the bottom border. Notice that these cover the narrowest part of the offset halo.

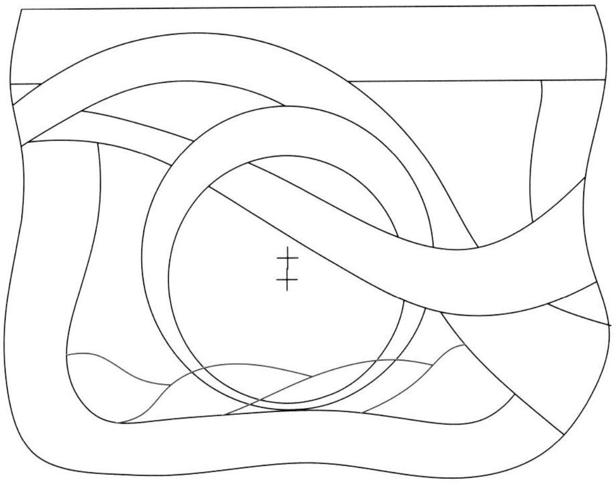

Draw lines for hills.

13. Erase the portion of the halo that is behind the rolling hills.

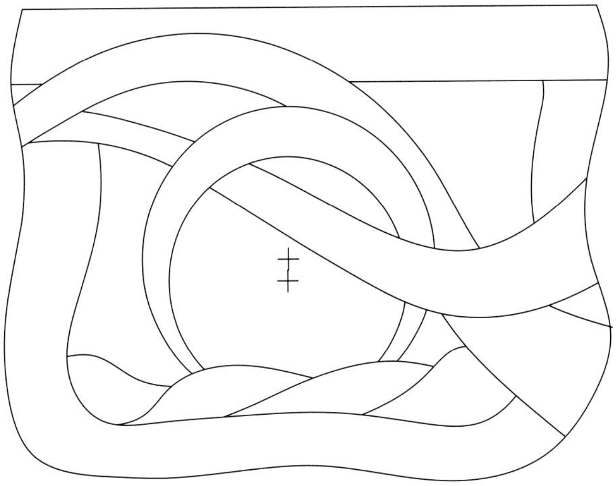

Erase unnecessary lines.

14. Use the flexible curve to audition and draw lines for tiny trees. I generally make at least 2 trees in a design because it adds balance and interest. Notice that I positioned the left tree so it covered even more of the offset halo.

> **Note**
>
> *Drawing tiny trees is similar to drawing flying geese (page 21), except that the angled sides of the trees do not meet in the center and rather than having angled basic brickwork (page 20), these lines are horizontal throughout each tree. The topmost section will be one solid piece of tree fabric.*

15. Draw horizontal brickwork lines inside the tree sections, and then draw the angled lines.

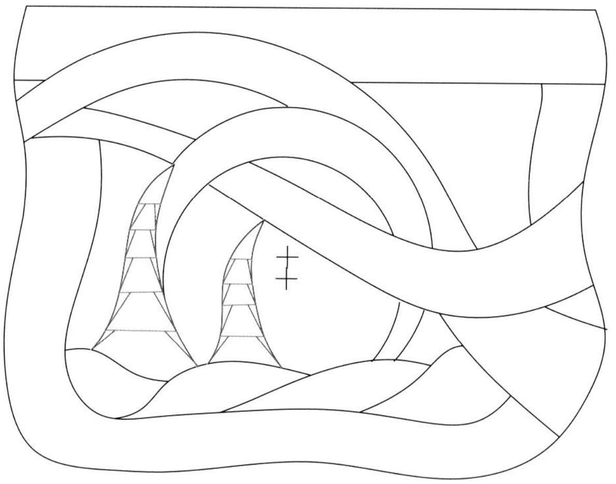

Draw curved lines for trees. Draw brickwork and interior angled lines in trees to finish tiny trees design.

FILLERS

Fill the free-form shapes with any filler you like (pages 20–33), or leave some of the shapes as solid pieces of fabric. The illustrations below show you some options.

1. To fill the halo, use the second center X you made to draw the halo and a straight-edge ruler to divide the halo into approximately equal sections. Pivot the ruler around the center point to create as many divisions as you want. This forms a basic brickwork pattern, which can be used to create many other fillers. It would also be effective as is, filled with gradating fabrics.

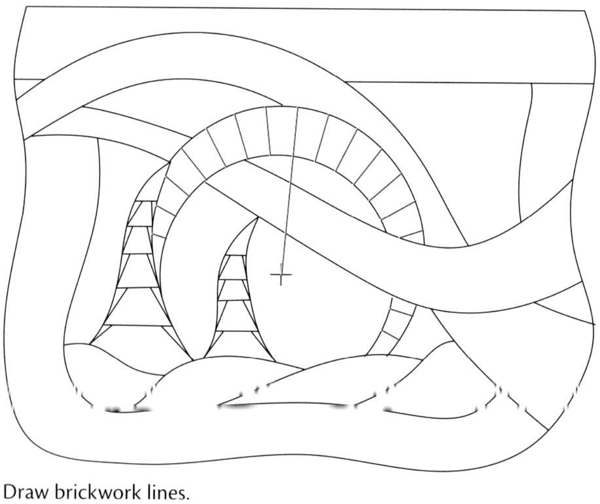

Draw brickwork lines.

2. Using the basic brickwork, create dashing sunrays (page 24). I chose to show them going in opposite directions from the top center.

Draw angled lines and erase unnecessary lines.

3. Draw pointy dudes (page 30) in the top border strip.

Draw pointy dudes in top border.

Note

In order to draw a pointy dudes border that disappears behind the filler strip, it is necessary to first draw the entire border as it would appear if it were on top of the strip and then erase some lines.

4. Erase the unnecessary brickwork and border lines.

Note

Sometimes you will need to change a few of the lines to make it easier to sew. Before finalizing a drawing, I review and simplify areas as much as possible to reduce the number of different foundations necessary to complete the quilt top.

5. Draw 10,000 pyramids (page 24) in the curved border. Notice that the corners must have narrow outward-facing pyramids and wide inward-facing pyramids.

Erase unnecessary lines in top border. Then, draw 10,000 pyramids in curved border.

6. Fill in the final 2 shapes with flying geese (page 21). Note that where 1 strip disappears behind the other, the geese are offset to enhance the illusion.

Draw flying geese in remaining 2 filler strips.

At this point, I would consider the design to be complete. However, it is fairly complex, relative to its overall size. This is the time to take it to your local photocopy shop and have it enlarged to a size that is easier to sew.

Another Option—Sunrise

1. To create the illusion of a sunrise in the background, select a point somewhere beyond the horizon of your design and draw radiating lines from that point to simulate the rays of the sun.

Draw radiating lines.

2. Erase the lines that disappear behind another design element.

Erase unnecessary lines.

Fillers: The Space between the Lines

Most of the designs in this book begin with a collection of gracefully flowing lines that are filled with design elements that complement the flowing curves. Perhaps the most obvious is the flying goose shape.

For these drafting exercises, you will need several letter-sized pieces of paper, a flexible curve, a mechanical pencil, a good eraser, and a 1″ × 6″ ruler.

These drafting exercises start with this basic shape: Use the flexible curve to draw two flowing, curved lines that are narrow on one side of the paper and widen into a graceful, downward-curving swoop on the other side of the paper. Think of this as the road that you will fill with wonderfully different designs described in the following sections. Converting these designs into foundation-piecing patterns is covered in Freezer-Paper Foundation Piecing (pages 44–53).

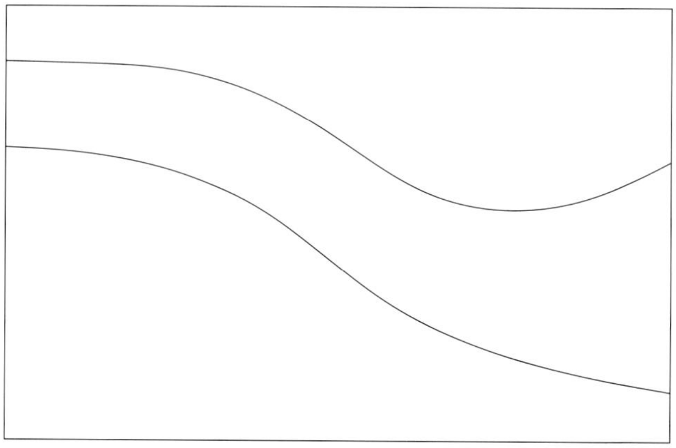

Draw 2 curved lines.

Brickwork

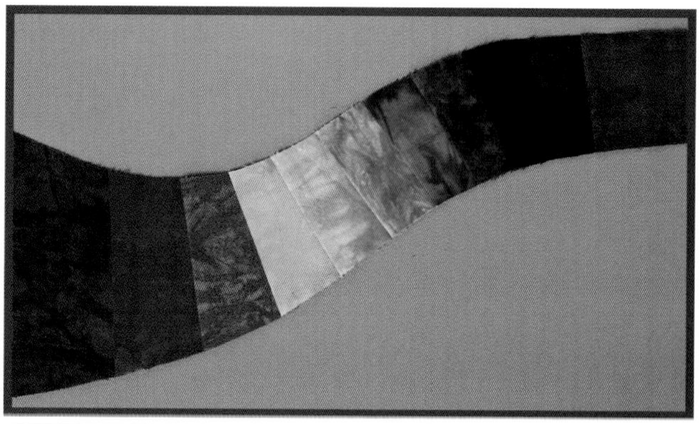

Brickwork is the foundation from which most other designs evolve. It can be quite effective as a filler, particularly when using hand-dyed fabric gradations. To visualize how to divide the "road" into sections that allow for the inclusion of more complex designs, I like to refer to it as the "yellow brick road." Pave the road with bricks, using only straight lines. To get around the curved sections, angle the lines so they are roughly perpendicular to the outside lines of the road.

1. Draw your first perpendicular brickwork line on a section of the road that is mostly straight.

2. Then, work toward an outer edge making, each additional brick about the same proportion as its neighbor.

3. Once you've reached the end of the road, turn the paper around and fill in the other end of the road.

I generally choose to make individual bricks that are wider (the distance between the two curves) than they are tall. The most important quality is that they are consistent. As the road widens, you will need to make the dividing lines a little farther apart, maintaining the overall proportion and enhancing the illusion of nearness. Similarly, as the road narrows into the distance, the dividing lines should be closer together.

4. Number the pieces sequentially in preparation for paper-foundation piecing.

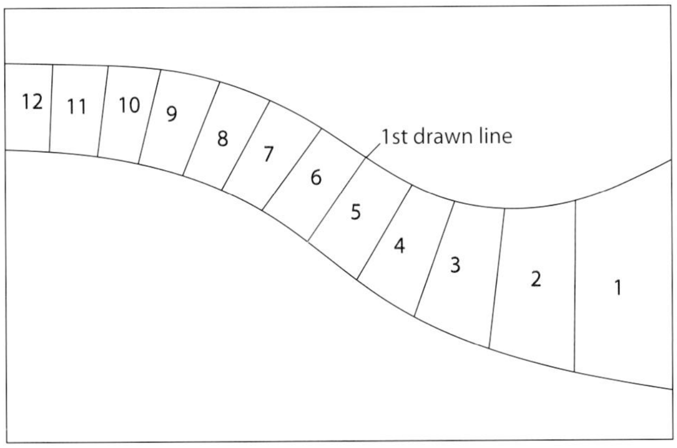

Draw brickwork and number.

tip

Brickwork can be stitched from either end. In general, it is easier to paper-foundation piece beginning at the widest end of a long strip.

Flying Geese

This may be one of the most versatile design elements. It works well with different-colored fabric scraps, incorporating fabrics from elsewhere in the design, and with hand-dyed gradations that allow the road to undulate across the design. It also works well with a beautiful hand-painted fabric in which the pattern changes slowly throughout the length of the road, with vibrant rainbow-printed fabrics, or with fabrics that change from a light to a dark shade or even several shades.

1. Draw brickwork.

2. Use a flexible curve to audition and draw a line that roughly divides the road in half down its length. This centerline will align the points of the geese.

3. Fill in the goose shapes. It doesn't matter which direction the geese point.

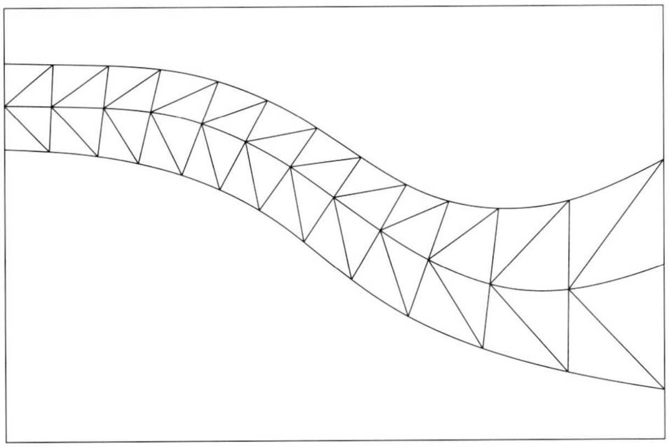

Draw brickwork and add curved centerline. Then, draw geese.

4. Erase the centerline.

5. Number the pieces sequentially.

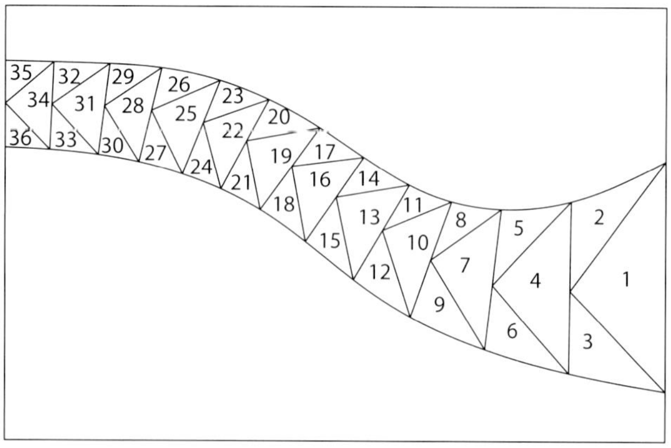

Erase centerline and number pieces.

This design can only be paper pieced in one direction, starting at the end with the widest part of the goose and adding pieces as you work along the strip, in the general direction in which the geese point (see Stitching the Strips, pages 49–52.).

tip

Numbering the piecing order of each foundation will reduce mistakes.

Off-Center Flying Geese

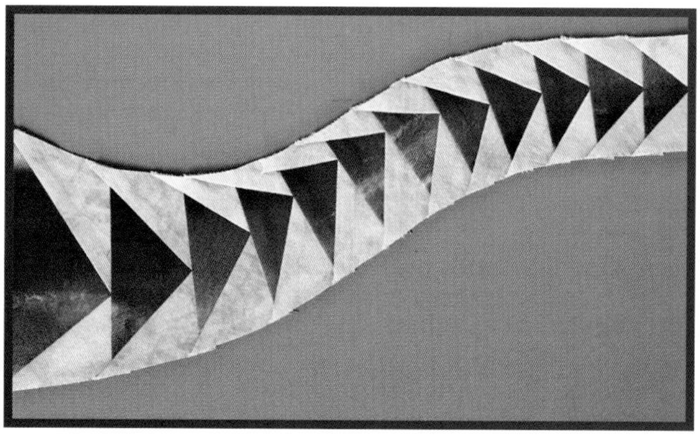

This is one of the fun variations of flying geese. It gives a very different look to the design, and yet still maintains the illusion of flying geese.

1. Draw brickwork (page 20) and add a curved off-center line angled off toward one side of the road.

2. Draw the goose shapes, like the standard flying goose strip (page 21).

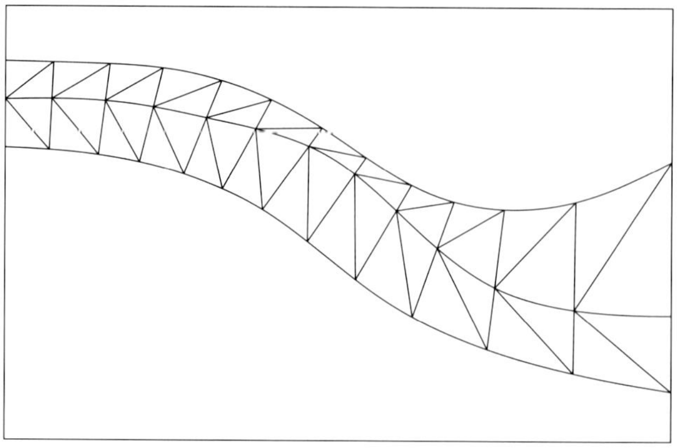

Draw brickwork and add curved off-center line. Then, draw geese.

3. Erase the center line. Number the pieces and assemble in the same manner as flying geese.

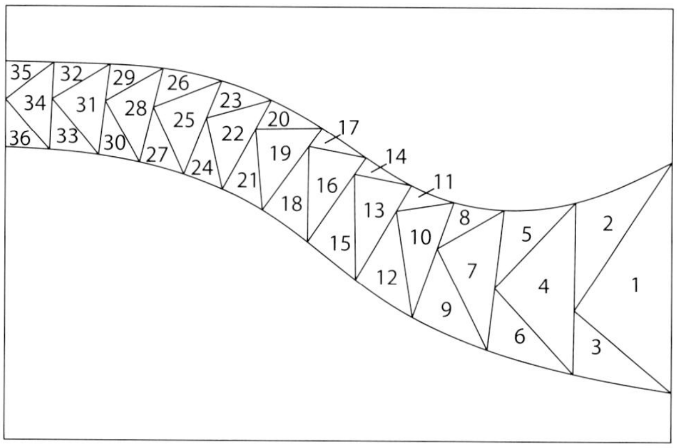

Erase off-center line. Then, number pieces.

Geese That Slide off the Edge!

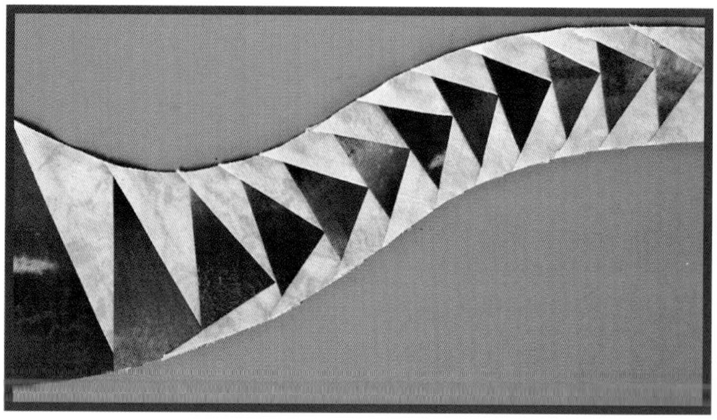

Yikes! Is it possible that the geese got to flying so fast they slid right off the edge of the road?

1. Draw brickwork (page 20) and add a curved off-center line that slides to one side and then angles completely off the other side of the road. Be sure that the transition is gentle. This creates an interesting illusion in which a flying geese design transitions into another design that I call Dashing Sunrays (page 24). If your overall quilt design is large, you can use geese in part of the road, transition to long, thin points, and then return to geese. It is indeed a fun and exciting filler.

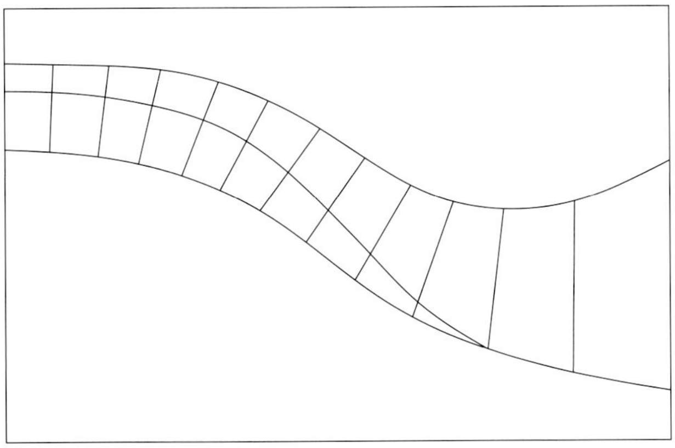

Draw brickwork and add curved line that slides to one side and then off other side.

2. Draw the geese shapes, like the standard flying geese strip (page 21), and erase the off-center line.

3. Number the pieces and assemble in the same manner as flying geese (page 49).

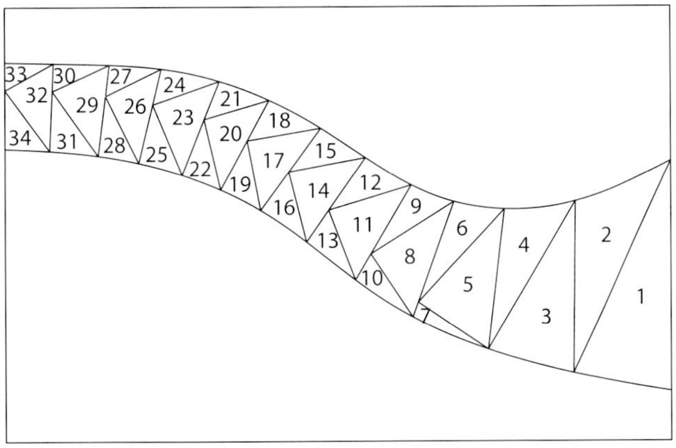

Draw geese shapes and number pieces.

Picket Fence

Picket fence is essentially one-half of flying geese.

1. Draw brickwork (page 20).

2. Draw a centerline down the length of the road. Then, draw a line from the center point to the outer edge on one side only.

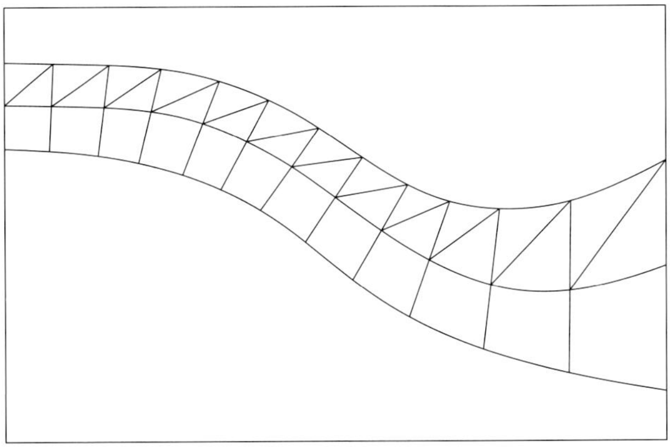

Draw centerline; then draw lines from center point to outer edge.

3. Erase the centerline and number the pieces.

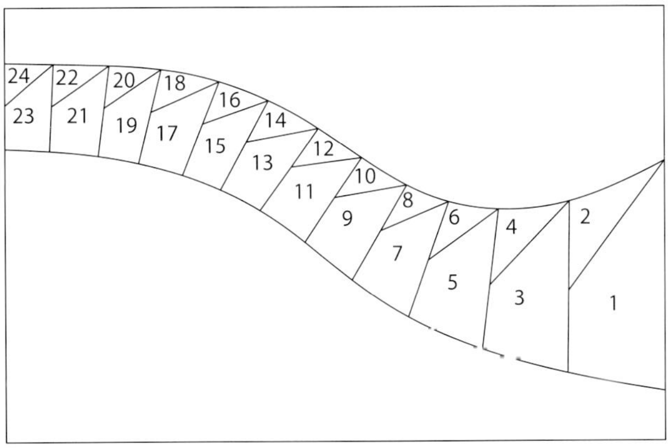

Erase centerline and number pieces sequentially.

4. Paper piece in the same manner as flying geese (page 49).

10,000 Pyramids

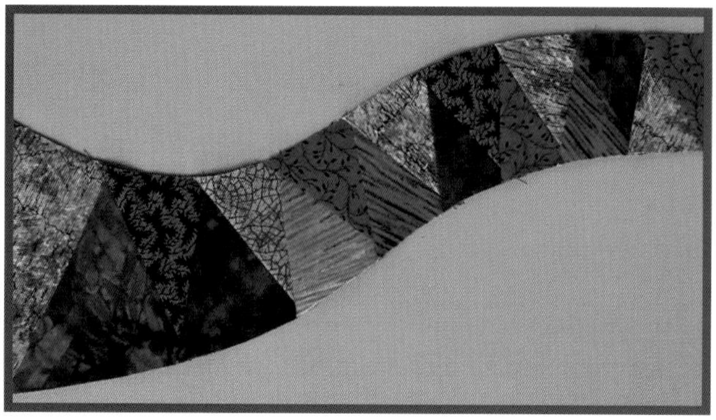

This filler is, without a doubt, one of my favorites and is incredibly versatile. The beauty of this strip lies in the two distinctly different designs that can be created. The most obvious is a basic sunray design with a light color on one side and a contrast on the alternate triangle. However, this design shimmers when filled with a wide variety of scraps, all of the same colorway. It also can be used for a background or anywhere you desire subtle background motion in your quilt.

> **tip**
>
> *Piece this filler strip with fabrics that gradate from light to dark and back for a three-dimensional look, or with many different fabrics of the same color. Reds can make a dramatic statement.*

1. With a 1″ × 6″ ruler, draw an angular line that forms a triangle at one end of the curved strip. Stop drawing when the line reaches the other side of the strip, pivot the ruler to form another triangle, and then draw the line to the original side of the strip. Continue on in this fashion until the entire strip is filled with triangles. I tend to make fairly wide triangles to reduce the number of pieces in this filler. If you prefer to make long, narrow triangles, refer to Dashing Sunrays (below).

All the triangles will be slightly different sizes because the width of the strip and the curves vary. Enjoy the asymmetry of it all.

2. Number the pieces. It is very simple to paper piece using the technique described in Stitching the Strips (pages 49–52).

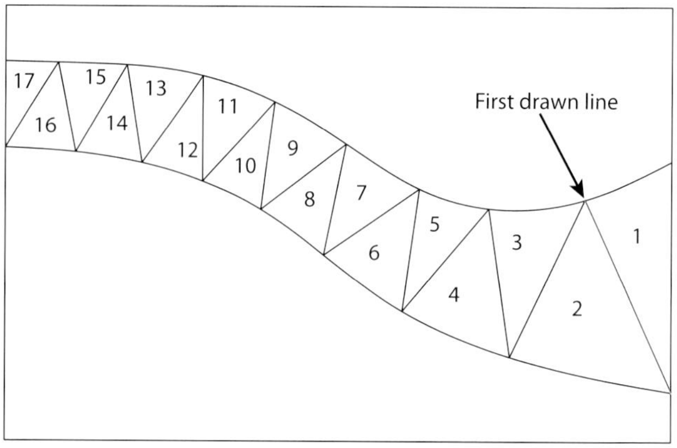

Draw 2 curved lines and connect with straight lines. Number pieces.

Dashing Sunrays

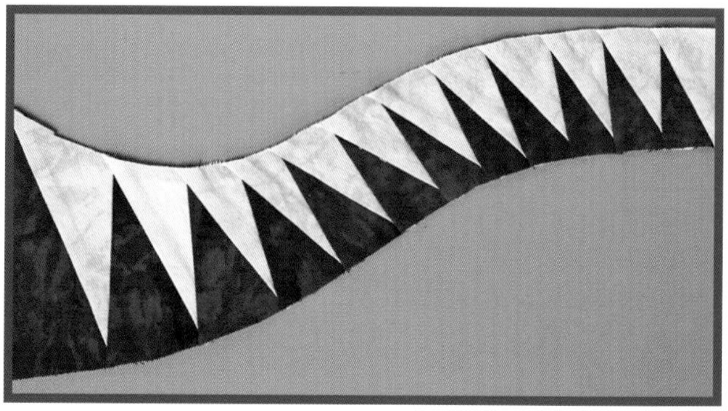

This border is similar to 10,000 pyramids (above) except the triangular divisions are much narrower, creating the look of zigzags throughout the strip. I generally use two highly contrasting fabrics to accentuate the starkness of this pattern. Paper piece in the same manner as 10,000 Pyramids.

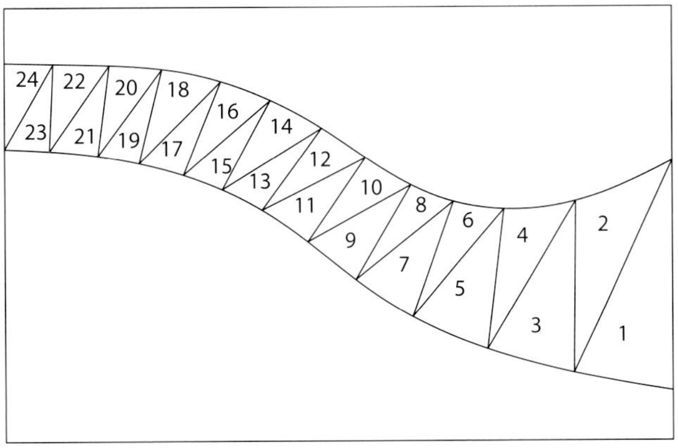

Draw 2 curved lines and connect them with straight lines.
Number pieces.

Mountains and Valleys

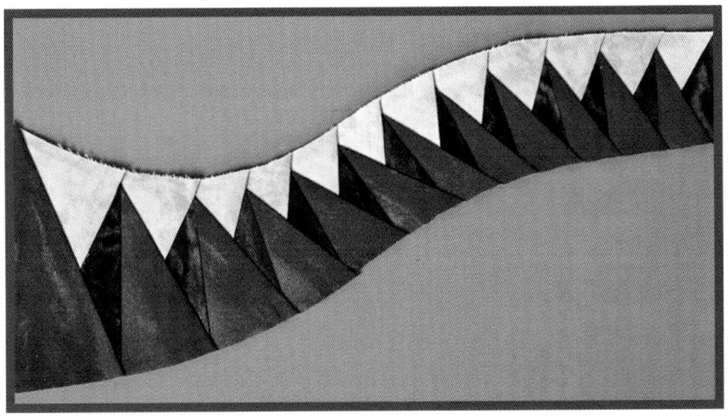

This lovely design can be very effective within the body of a quilt top and as an outer border. Strong contrast between the mountain peaks (lighter shade) and the valleys (darker shade) is essential.

1. Draw dashing sunrays (page 24).

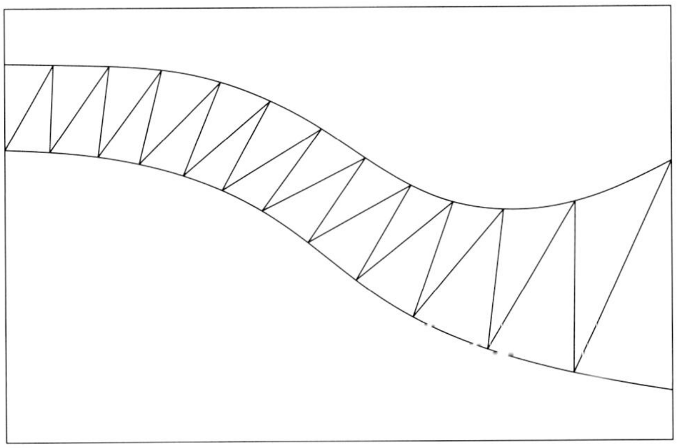

Draw 2 curved lines and connect them with straight lines.

2. Draw a second set of lines from opposite corners that cross the original lines.

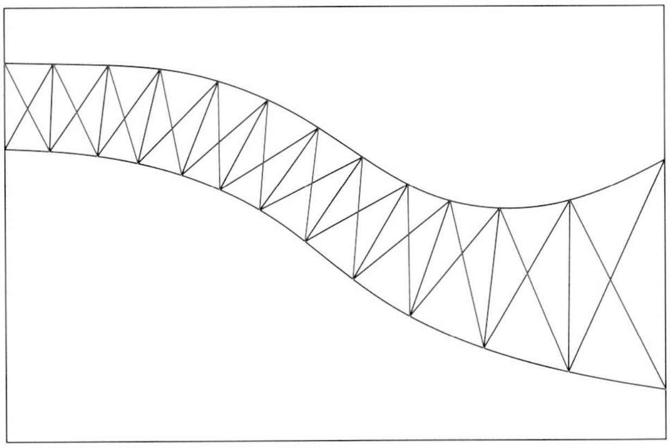

Draw second set of lines (red) opposite of original lines.

3. Erase the portions of the lines that extend beyond the original lines.

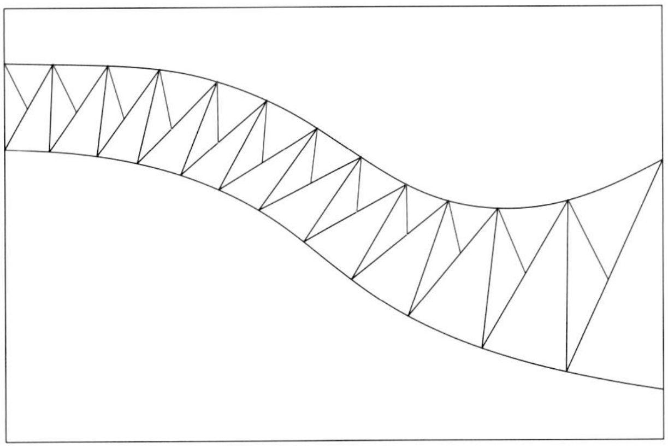

Erase unnecessary lines.

tip

Another option is to simply stop drawing the lines that will extend beyond the original lines.

4. Number the pieces sequentially. This design can be paper pieced (pages 49–52) in only one direction because of the placement of the mountain's shadow.

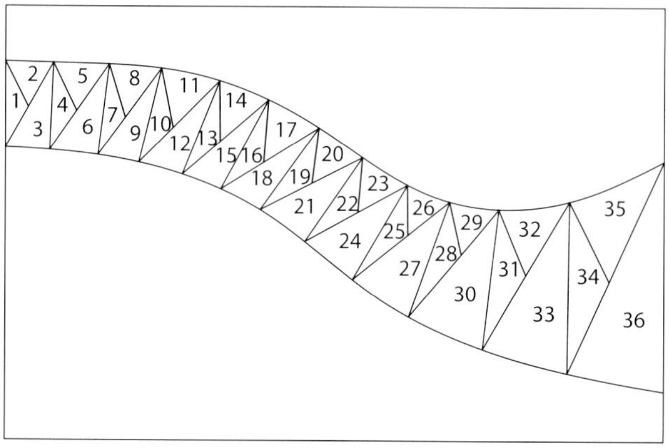

Number pieces.

Spirals

The spirals filler lends itself well to using hand-dyed gradations. It is based on the brickwork design.

1. Draw brickwork (page 20).

2. Draw a line that extends across 2 bricks, from the lower left corner of the first brick in the strip to the opposite end of the second brick, forming a point at the end. Repeat, starting at the lower left corner of the second brick, and then continuing on.

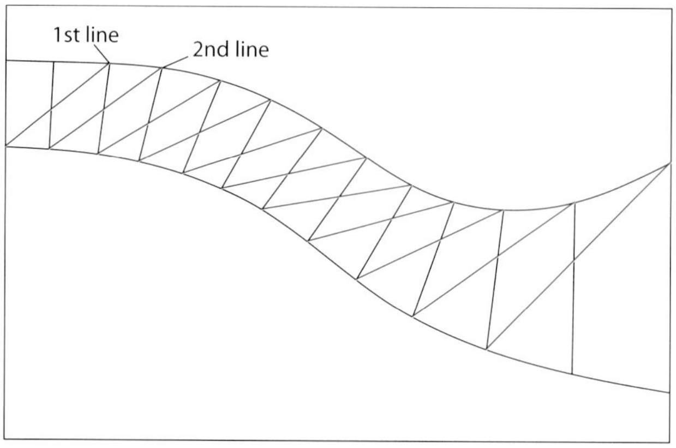

Draw brickwork. Then, draw lines to form points.

3. Erase the original brickwork lines and add an additional line to each end of the filler, if needed, so it appears that the design continues beyond the boundaries of this strip.

4. Number the pieces.

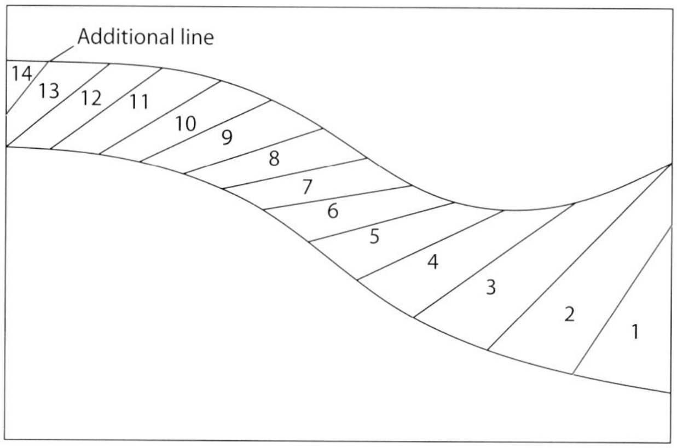

Erase original brickwork lines and add lines as needed. Number pieces.

This is a simple block to paper piece and can be pieced from either end (pages 49–52).

Braid

The braid pattern might seem complex but is actually rather simple to draw. It is based on the basic brickwork pattern.

1. Draw brickwork (page 20).

2. Starting at one end of the strip, mark a point that is about midway between the 2 sides of the filler. Crossing over 2 brick sections, draw a very tall triangle (shown in red). Then, from the lower right side of the third brick in the filler, draw a line that ends at the intersection of the first brick and first triangle (shown in green). Draw another line that starts at the upper right side of this third brick and ends at the other intersection point of the first brick and the first triangle.

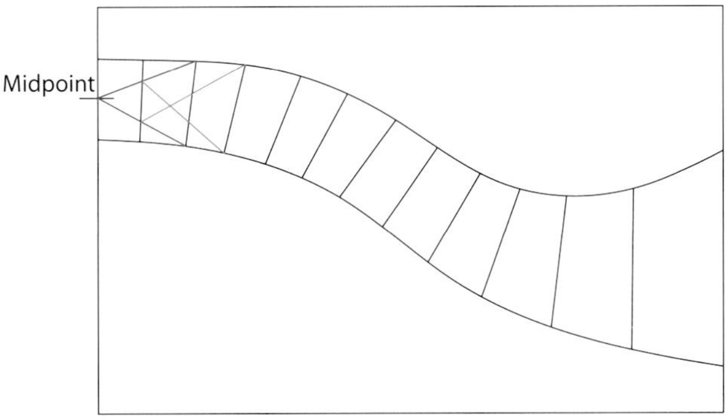

Draw brickwork. Then, mark midway point and draw triangles.

3. Continue drawing these lines until you reach the opposite end of the filler. Add additional lines at the end of the filler, so it appears that the design continues beyond the strip boundaries.

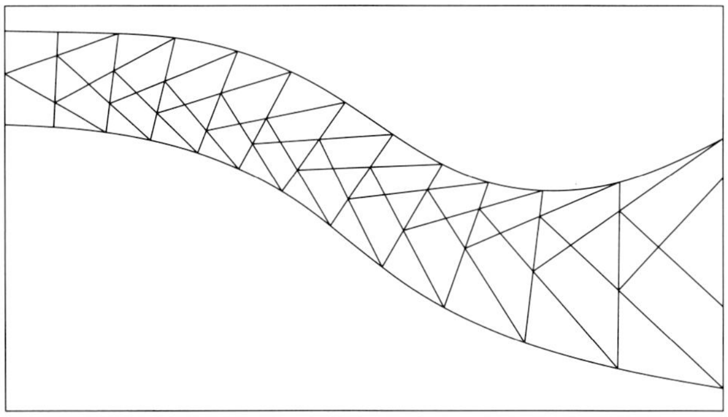

Draw lines to opposite end.

4. Erase 1 of the lines that extends beyond the newly formed triangle. Repeat down the length of the strip, erasing the same partial line in each brick.

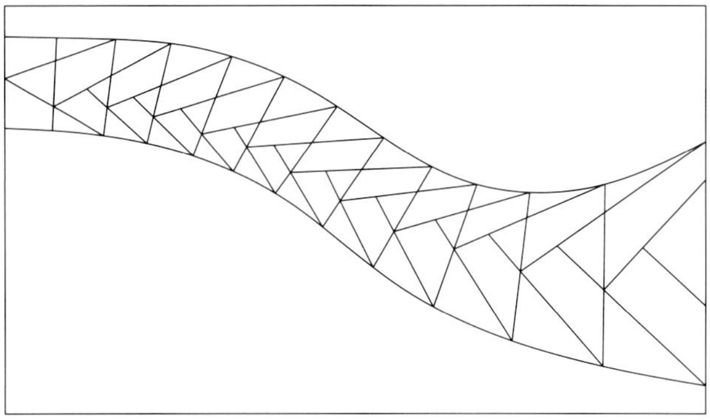

Erase partial lines.

5. Erase the brickwork lines, leaving a braid. Draw another set of lines at each end, if needed, so that the design appears to continue beyond the boundaries of this strip, and number the pieces.

6. Number the pieces.

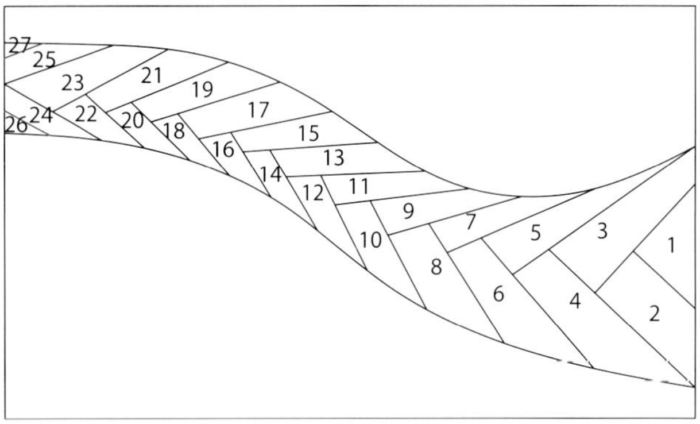

Erase brickwork lines and add lines at one end. Number pieces.

This pattern is easily paper pieced starting from one end (pages 49–52).

Migrating Geese

This wonderful design was created by Nancy Durand of Wasilla, Alaska. She generously offered to share this offset flying geese design.

1. Draw brickwork (page 20).

2. Draw 2 lines down the length of the road, dividing the bricks into thirds.

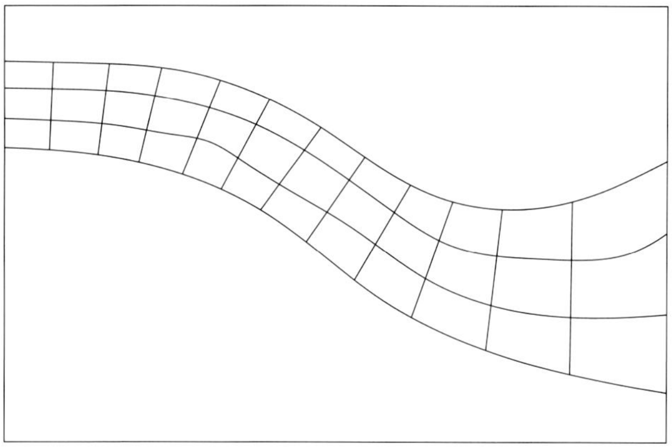

Draw brickwork. Then, draw 2 lines.

3. Beginning at the upper left corner of the strip, draw the upper leg of a goose that is only as wide as ⅓ of that brick. Then, extend the lower leg so it reaches the lower edge of the next brick (shown in red).

4. Then, from the intersection of the lower leg of the first goose with the first brick, draw a line that extends to the upper right corner of the third brick (green).

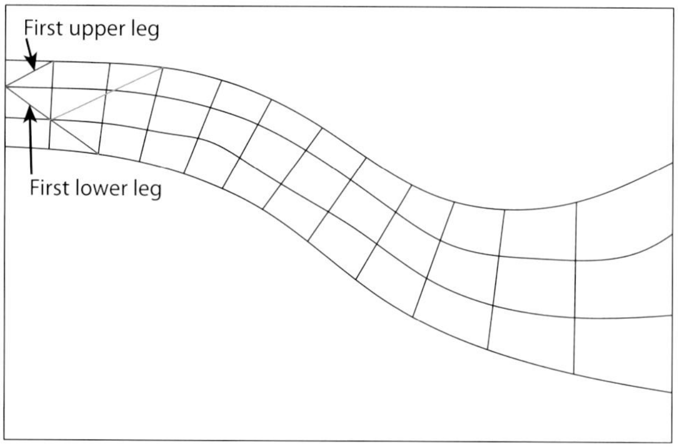

Draw lines.

5. Moving down the strip, continue adding lines in this fashion until you reach the end of the brickwork strip.

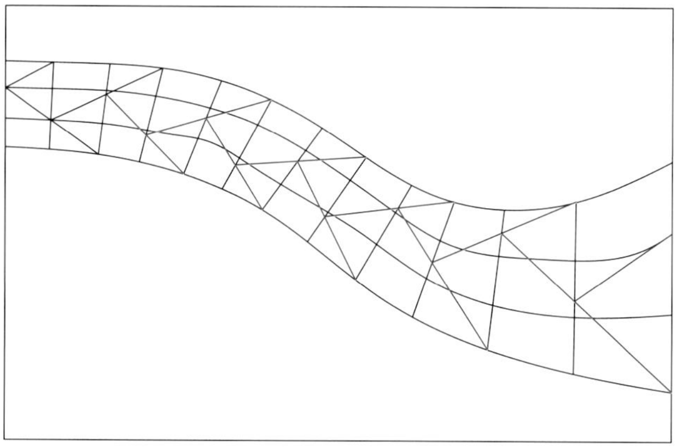

Continue drawing lines.

Notice that the geese are *not* always aligned with the original 2 dividing lines. This is okay. The final design will have proportionally correct geese.

6. Erase the 2 dividing lines that run lengthwise.

7. Then erase the brickwork lines that extend beyond the end of the geese.

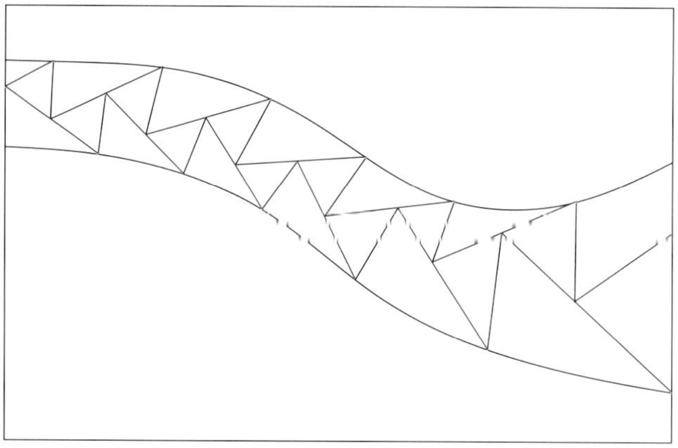

Erase extra lines.

8. Number the pieces.

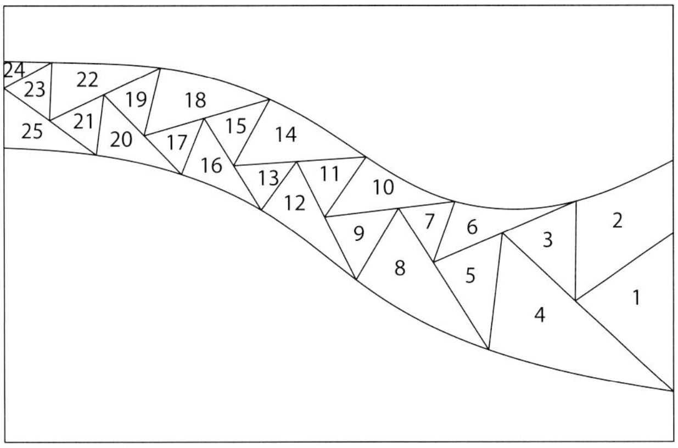

Number pieces.

The pattern is slightly more challenging to paper piece (pages 49–52), but the overall effect is well worth the extra effort.

Horizontal Pointy Dudes

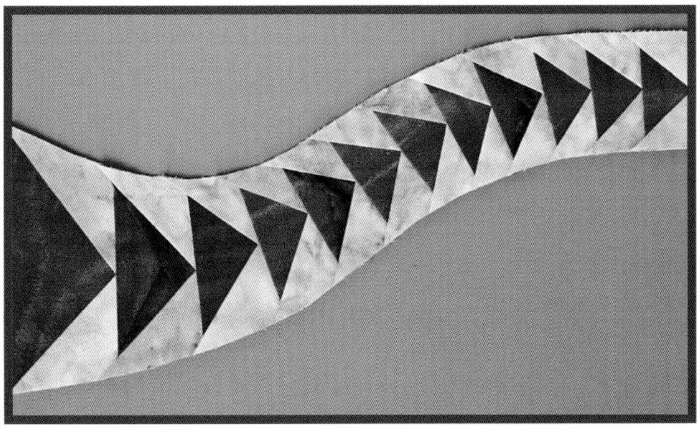

Pointy dudes (shown above in black) are a wonderful accent to any row of flying geese. Their effect in a quilt is like an arrow that directs the viewer's eye to a particular detail, or connects the center to a border, or even helps the viewer see the flow of the quilt design. Be sure to use a fabric with strong contrast for your "dude." Lime green, red, and bright yellow can work well for pointy dudes.

1. Draw flying geese (page 21).

2. Pick out a goose that will benefit from a "dude." Draw a line from the top corner of the goose, angling it toward the opposite corner of the brickwork that is the basis for the goose design (red). However, the dude can be as wide as you desire.

3. Then, from the opposite side of the goose, draw an opposing line that stops before it crosses the first dude line.

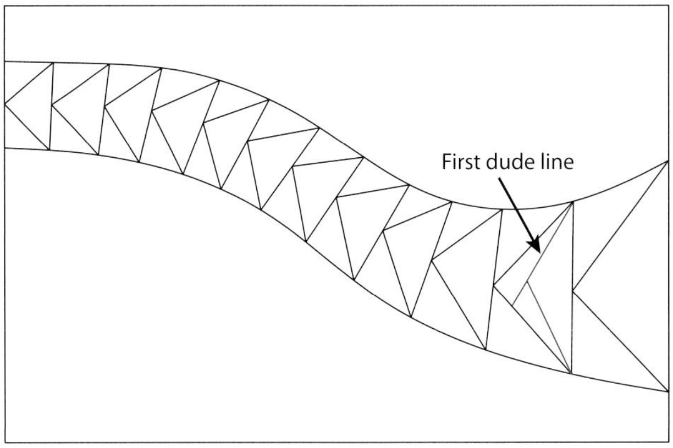

Draw flying geese. Draw pointy dude lines.

4. Draw a few more. *In the case of pointy dudes, less is more.* In general, I use them only once in a while, for effect.

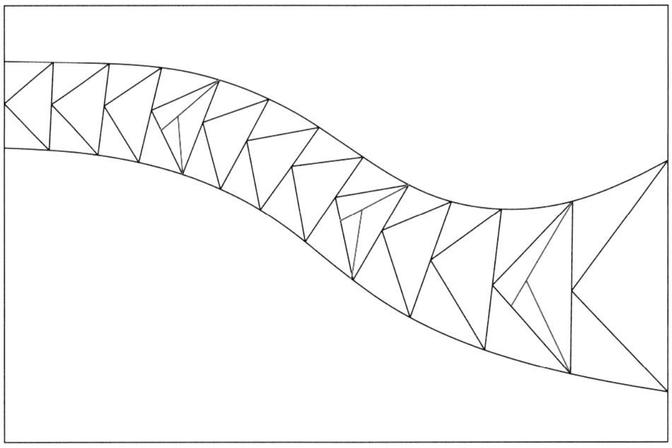

Draw a few more.

Note

Including only a few dudes has two benefits. The first is that there is less piecing. The second is that this accent gets lost if it is used on each goose and is less effective in your overall design. Dudes also are more effective when they appear in the larger geese, where they can be drawn a little wider. Narrow dudes and tiny dudes tend to disappear into a design. If you choose to use this element, make it a strong statement. Horizontal pointy dudes are pieced in the general order of a flying geese strip (pages 49–52).

5. Number the pieces.

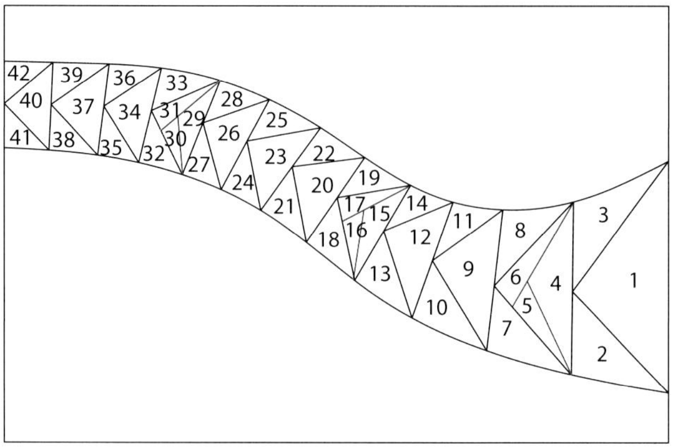

Number pieces.

Vertical Pointy Dudes in a Straight Setting

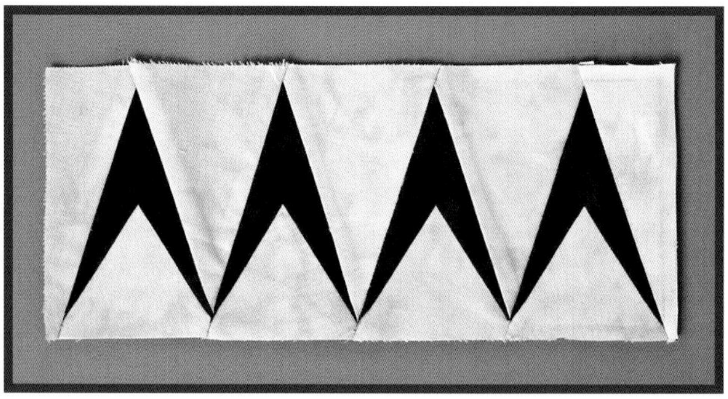

Be sure to use strongly contrasting fabrics to get the best effect from this design.

When horizontal pointy dudes (page 29) are turned 90°, they make a dramatic statement in a design. Vertical pointy dudes are most dramatic when they are tall and narrow. They are effective in both a straight-line setting, as in a border, or in a curved setting within a design. This type of pointy dude design is created differently from the other fillers we have explored so far. Follow the instructions carefully step by step.

1. Draw a basic grid that is taller than it is wide. A pleasing proportion might be a 3″-wide border divided into 1″-wide bricks.

2. Draw tall triangles.

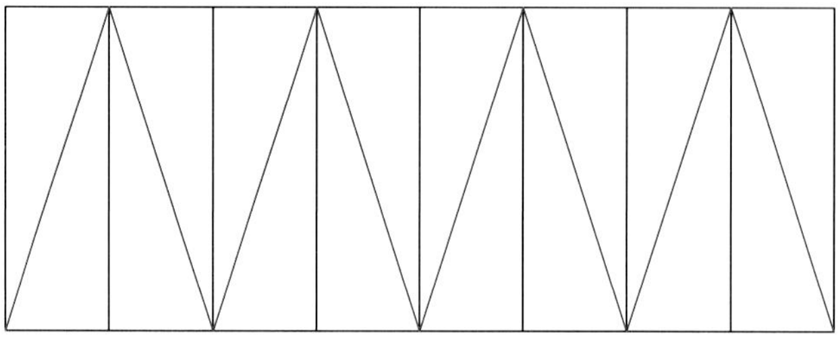

Draw grid; then draw triangles.

3. From the lower edges of the triangles, draw a line that extends to the upper corner of the next brick (red).

4. Repeat by drawing a line in the opposite direction, but stop drawing before crossing any lines (green).

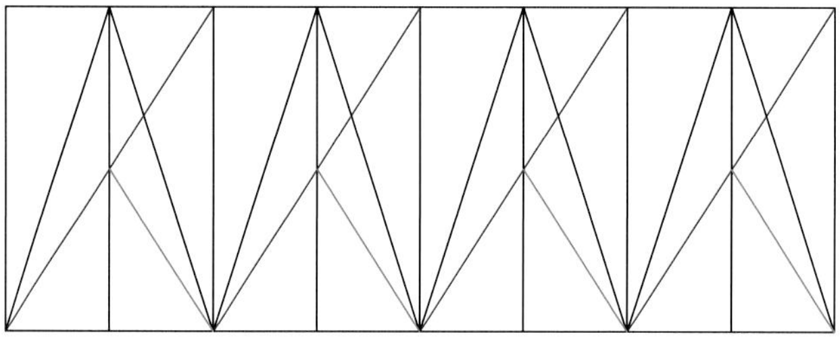

Draw more lines.

5. Erase the lines that extend beyond the triangles.

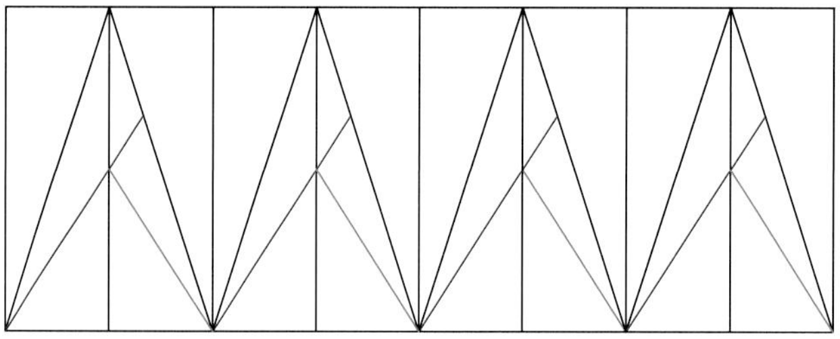

Erase extending lines.

6. Erase all remaining brickwork lines.

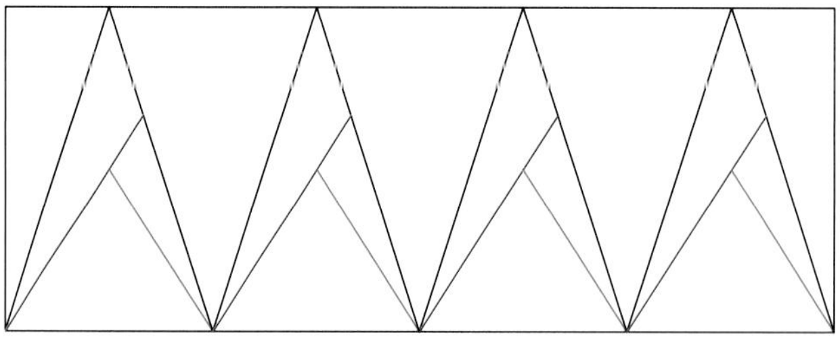

Erase grid lines.

The vertical pointy dudes filler is assembled differently from all other fillers. It can only be paper pieced in short sections that are then stitched together to form the straight filler. It also is necessary to make a template pattern for the ends of each straight border.

7. Number the filler pieces and make the end template patterns.

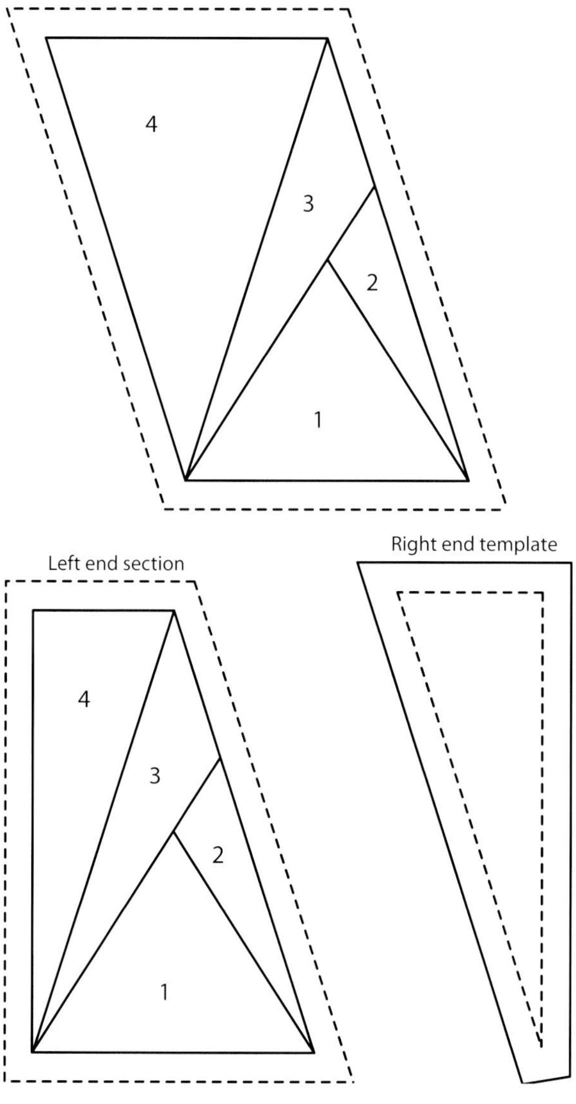

Number pieces and make repeating foundations and end template patterns.

Vertical Pointy Dudes in a Curved Setting

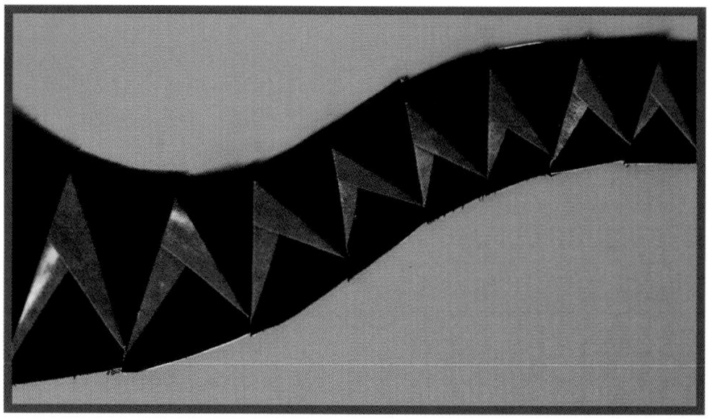

Vertical pointy dudes in a curved setting are similar to those in a straight-edge setting (page 30), but with a few differences.

1. Draw brickwork (page 20) and keep the bricks narrow, about 1″ wide and 3″ tall.

2. Draw tall triangles.

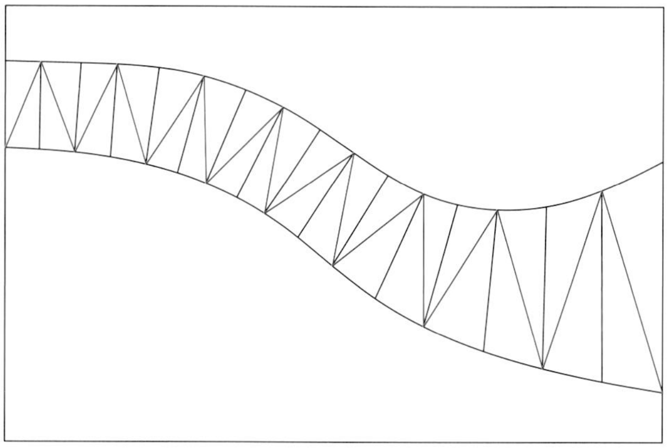

Draw brickwork; then draw triangles.

3. From the lower edges of the triangles, draw a line that extends to the upper corner (red) of the next brick.

4. Repeat by drawing a line in the opposite direction, but stop drawing before crossing any lines (shown in green, next illustration).

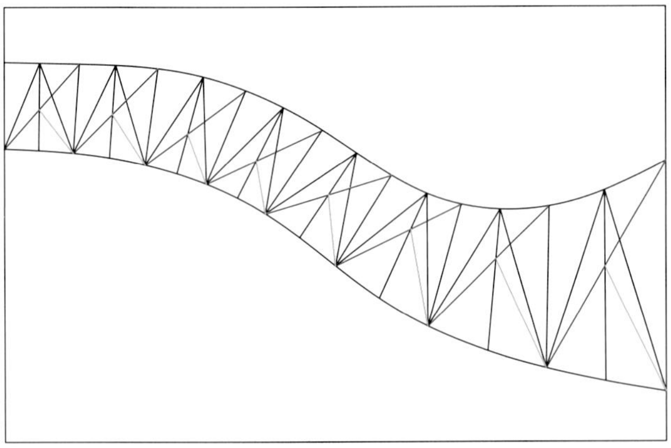

Draw more lines.

5. Erase the extra lines, including all lines outside the pointy dudes and the inside brickwork lines.

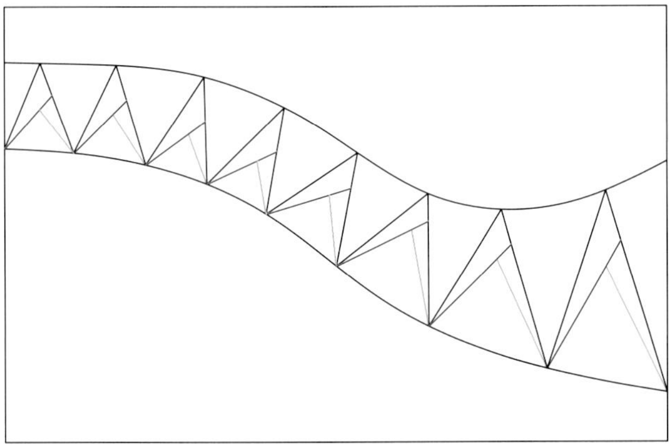

Erase extra lines.

Notice that as the filler strip gets wider toward the right edge, the legs of the pointy dudes get much narrower.

When this happens, redraw the legs of the dudes to match the proportion of the other pointy dudes in the filler strip and then erase the original pointy dude legs.

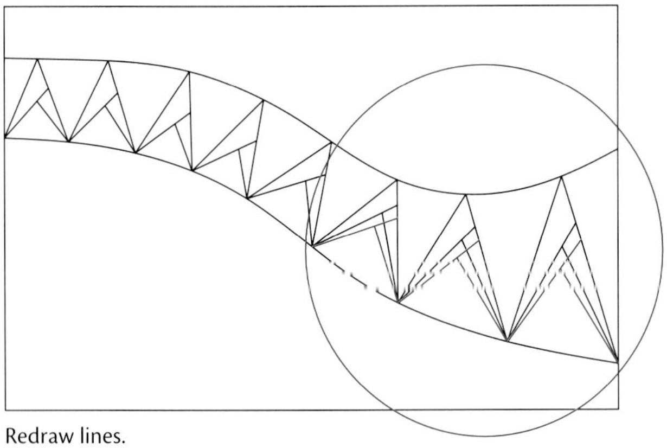

Redraw lines.

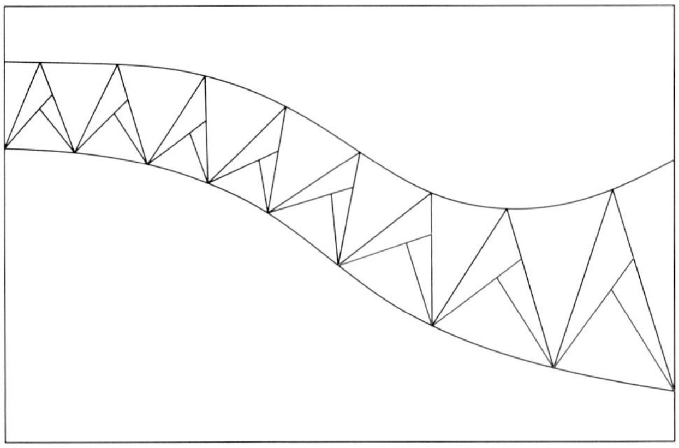

Erase extra lines.

Curved pointy dudes can only be assembled in short sections that are then stitched together. Because the adjacent sections are quite similar in size and shape, it is a good idea to number each separate dude foundation and also mark the top of each section. This will prevent you from accidentally stitching an upside-down section into the filler strip.

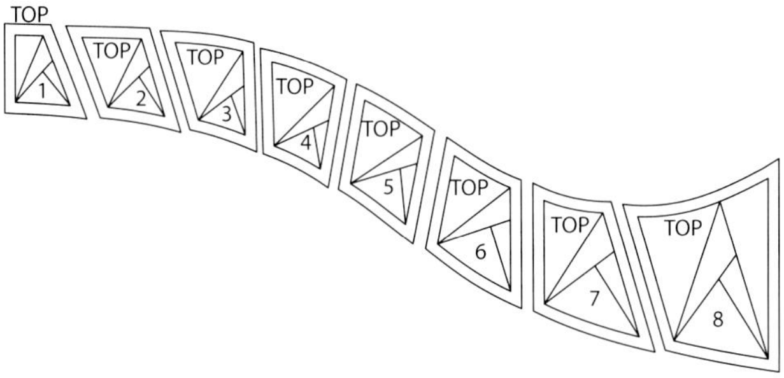

Number each section and mark top.

All of the pointy dude foundations will be similar except for the 2 end pieces, and each will be stitched in the same manner (pages 49–52). Note that the shapes on the outer edge pieces are different, and the right end has 5 pieces instead of 4.

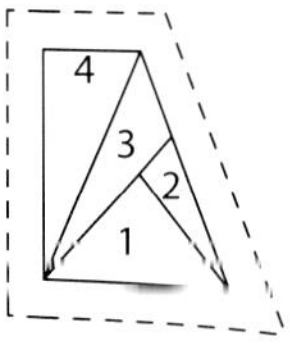

Left end pattern

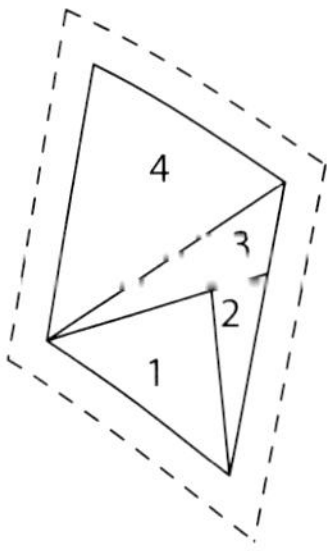

Interior pattern

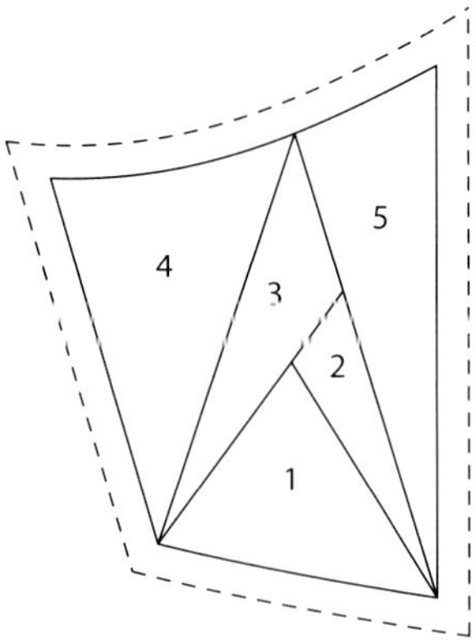

Right end pattern

Flying Diamonds

Flying diamonds is a filler that works well as a base for other designs that are combinations of flying geese, flying diamonds, and pointy dudes (as shown in Designing with Free-Form Shapes, pages 12–19).

1. Draw brickwork (page 20) and keep the bricks narrower, about 1″ wide and 3″ tall.

2. Mark the center point of the brickwork lines. Draw a series of diamonds in the brickwork by connecting the center points to the corners as shown.

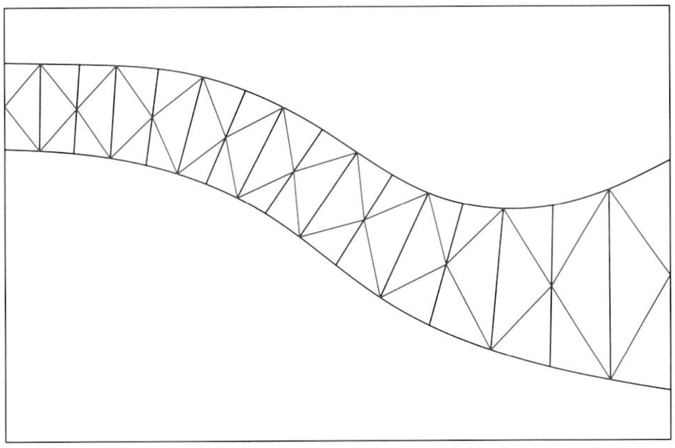

Draw brickwork; then draw diamonds.

3. Erase the brickwork lines in the middle of the diamonds.

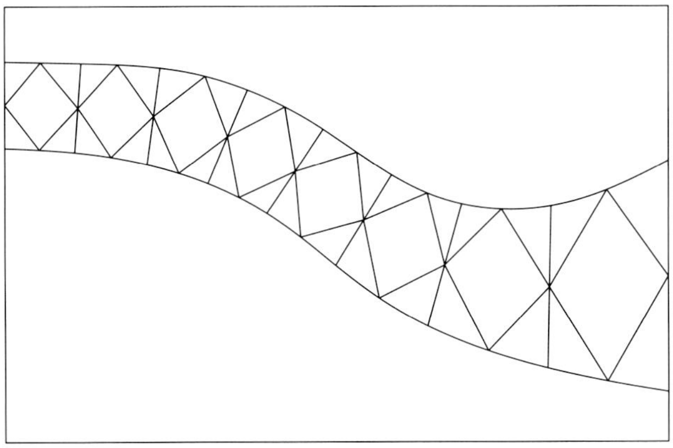

Erase lines.

Flying diamonds must be assembled as separate foundations that are then stitched together to form the filler strip. The design will not piece in a long row. Each foundation is assembled in the same manner. Number each separate foundation and mark the top of each section.

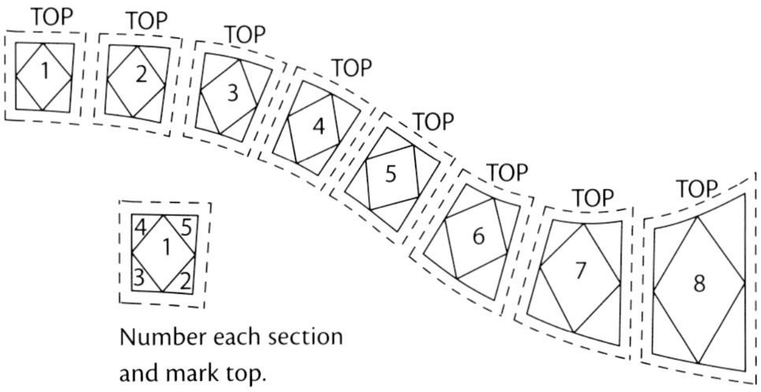

Number each section and mark top.

Color and Contrast

I have one common goal for each quilt that I make. If that quilt is displayed on the back wall of a large exhibit hall, then all of its elements—foreground, background, and borders—must be clearly visible from across a large room. This requires strong contrast between the different components. For this reason, I believe that contrast is more important than color. When I choose fabrics for a quilt, contrast is always uppermost in my mind for all areas that need to stand out. Most of my quilts include many different colors, and I often use rainbow gradations with every shade of the color wheel. But when I want something to stand out, I make sure that it *really* does. There are a variety of different ways to ensure that there is adequate contrast between those elements that should appear distinctly different, as discussed below.

Most of the fabrics in my stash are prints that read as solids. All are organized on floor-to-ceiling shelves arranged by colors. Over the years, those strongly textured fabrics that I once thought were so wonderful have migrated to the bottom of the stack. With my fabrics organized like this, I can clearly see when a stack is getting low and I need to go shopping for a particular color. To me, it is important to have a large fabric stash on hand. An assortment of twenty or so different purples might be just the thing that is needed to make a border or background stand out.

I'm also a huge fan of hand-dyed and hand-painted fabrics. I keep these fabrics separate from the others so I can easily find them. Most of my more recent quilts contain at least one of these specialty fabrics, and sometimes most of the quilt is made from them. I like to use gradations in my filler strips, and I love using hand-painted sky fabric as a strong statement in the background.

Sometimes, however, that very same hand-painted sky that was the inspiration for a design will overwhelm all the other elements. Such was the case in my quilt *Syn-crane-icity*.

Syn-crane-icity by Gail Garber, 2002, 19″ × 22″

The inspiration for this small quilt was a commercially printed fabric that featured cranes and geese in a marsh. I carefully selected a piece of Skydyes hand-painted sky fabric (Resources, page 79) for the background, and began putting the quilt together. It was only after I had assembled all parts of the center (without borders) that I hung it on my design wall and looked at it through the wrong end of my binoculars.

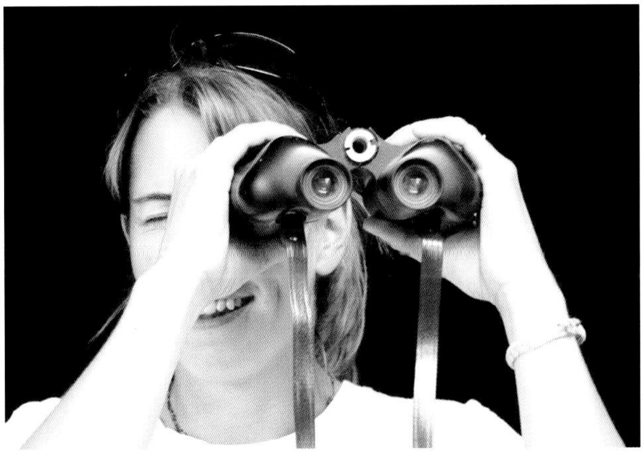

Look at quilt through wrong end of binoculars.

tip

Other tricks to help determine if there is enough contrast are to turn off the lights to look at the quilt in a semidarkened room, or hang the quilt where it can be seen from another room or at the end of a long hallway.

This binoculars trick makes the quilt look very far away, and I find it more effective than a reducing glass or peephole. I stepped back and took a look at my new masterpiece. Yikes! It looked like mush and everything blended together. Something had to be done! A repair was in order, and quickly, if the quilt was to be salvaged. So, I reevaluated my fabric choices and appliquéd new mountains right over the top of the old ones. It helped, but wasn't enough. So, I then resorted to a technique that I learned in 1984 from Fran Soika, a quiltmaker known for her Native American–inspired quilts. She taught me how to take one strand of black embroidery floss and, using either the backstitch or stem stitch, embroider around all the edges that need to have more contrast.

Embroidery to add contrast

Adding all that black is similar to the lines in a coloring book. It separates, defines, and automatically creates contrast between two fabrics that appear to be one from a distance.

When selecting fabrics for filler strips, I almost always choose a background fabric for that filler that is similar to but *distinctly different* from the primary background fabrics used in that quilt. This is evident in most of the quilts featured in this book. This was a lesson I learned the hard way. I was making a small sample to use in class that would show both curved and straight flying geese strips. I selected a Skydyes hand-dyed fabric and used it for both the primary background and the background behind the geese. Yeesh! It looked terrible. I never finished the top, but I use it all the time in my classes as a wonderful example of what not to do. I call it *Gridlock*.

Gridlock top

No matter how long we have been quilting, unfortunate fabric choices sometimes still haunt our quilts. Again, it all comes down to contrast. For the project quilt *Winding Ways* (page 75), I wanted the flying geese filler strips to appear as if they were weaving over and under throughout. I selected two shades of blue for the backgrounds of the fillers that I thought had enough contrast and set to stitching.

Blue fabrics

When I hung the top on the wall, it was immediately apparent that there was not enough contrast in the two blue backgrounds. The woven effect was not at all evident.

Not enough contrast in flying geese backgrounds to show woven effect

However, I wasn't about to give up on *Winding Ways*, which I thought had great potential. I certainly had no intention of starting over, either. *Winding Ways* had already been quilted and bound, but Donna and I decided to paint one of the fabrics to give it more contrast, using Shiva Artist's Paintstiks (Resources, page 79). We used a blue Paintstik to color in all the sections that would appear to be the lower part of the weave, and then used a brush to smooth out the paint and fill in the corners.

Applying Paintstik color

You be the judge of the finished project shown on page 75.

It's all about contrast! Next time you are at a quilt show, take a more critical look at those quilts that lack appeal to you. Is it the color that is disturbing? Or is it really the lack of contrast that makes those quilts less than pleasing?

I believe that contrast is the most important element in a quilt, but color also enters into the picture to a lesser degree. The right color for a certain spot can make or break a quilt. Just today, my friend Mary Chappelle came over to ask for advice on her latest project (completed project, *Night Flight over Water,* on page 59). It features the full moon reflecting on calm waters with geese migrating through the night sky. The problem was that because the sky and water were both dark in one area, it was impossible to distinguish between them. Mary had made the rounds of the local quilt shops and purchased several yards of different fabrics, none of which worked. So, we dove into my personal stash of hand-painted Skydyes and found the perfect sliver of pinkish-orange sunset that gave the illusion of the last sliver of sun at the end of the day before night settles in.

When I was a novice quilter nearly 30 years ago, another more experienced quilter told me that I should never use yellow because it would kill a quilt. It inspired me to immediately begin collecting yellows and oranges for a project! Although yellow is indeed a strong color, it is one of my favorites when used sparingly as an accent, particularly in the pointy dudes filler. Yellow (or, for that matter, lime green or purple) pointy dudes that contrast strongly with the other colors have the effect of directing the viewer's eye toward the element that you hope will be showcased in your design.

There also are times when contrast is not desirable, such as in the background of a design. To achieve the look of a cohesive background with multiple pieced sections, use fabric colors and values that are similar.

One of the best tips that I know of is to put your work up on a design wall as it develops. Stand back and take a good, hard look at the fabric choices. Be your own sternest critic. When you can't decide how to best proceed, just wait and let the quilt simmer quietly in the back of your subconscious. The answer will come to you when the time is right, and you'll be able to work on the project again. That's the beauty of patience.

Illusions

Flying geese and all its variations can be used to create a wonderful array of illusions, ranging from three-dimensional to whimsical. In this chapter we will explore ways to enrich your quilt designs.

Radiating Sunlight (or Moonlight)

The illusion of a light source radiating out from a central point within a design is what I call radiating sunlight or moonlight. It can be from the background of a star, as in my quilt *Black Hole*, or from a globe such as seen in the delightful quilt *Backyard Detective* by Lindy Filz (page 39). The basic flying geese design works well to achieve this illusion.

Black Hole by Gail Garber, 2002, 55″ × 50″
In the Collection of New Mexico Art in Public Places

Black Hole was an exercise in circular design. Although I started with circles to draft the undulating star, I used a curved line that ranged between concentric circles for the lines of the star and then erased all the original circles. My original goal was to create a background in shades of gray that radiated from light to dark; however, I quickly got bored working only in shades of gray, so I added a bright yellow pointy dude to liven things up. It was so successful that I continued adding pointy dudes throughout the background. In the end, the pointy dudes are the connection between the bright yellow center and the outer border.

This illusion is most effective in a larger design where there is enough space between the light source and the outer edge to allow the colors to change gradually. It can be enhanced by the addition of a few carefully placed pointy dudes that draw the viewer's eye toward the outer border and create an additional connection between the inner design, the background, and the border.

Detail of *Black Hole*

Backyard Detective by Lindy Filz, 2008, 40″ × 33″

Backyard Detective was inspired by Gail Garber's The Goose Is Loose class. The design began as a study in value. Even though I'm primarily a traditional quilter, the design became a personal challenge in developing an individual and whimsical style, which included my love of animals. —*Lindy*

Detail of *Backyard Detective;* radiating geese that create illusion of moonlight

Flip-Over Ribbon

The flipped-over ribbon gives a wonderful three-dimensional look in a quilt. However, it is one of the more challenging designs to draw. Think of a ribbon that is folded over on itself, and how the colors change when one part of the ribbon is in the shadow while the other side emerges into the light. I used this feature in my quilt *Galactic Tango* (page 41).

1. Draw 2 parallel lines that narrow toward the end that will flip over. Draw a second set of lines that appear to come from behind and flip over the top and then cross at the other end. Erase the underlying lines.

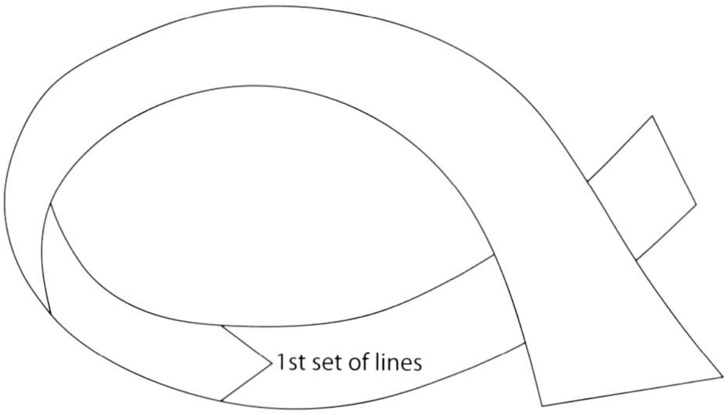

Draw 2 sets of parallel lines. Erase unnecessary lines.

Both sets of lines are narrower toward the flip, but they do not form an absolute X where it changes direction. Although this area is narrower than the full width of the ribbon, there is always some thickness at this point. For this particular shape, I only fill the strip with geese formed with a center dividing line within the strip.

2. Draw the center dividing line for the geese.

Notice that the distance between the midpoint and the inner side of both fillers remains the same, but that the outer portion gets thinner as it approaches the flip.

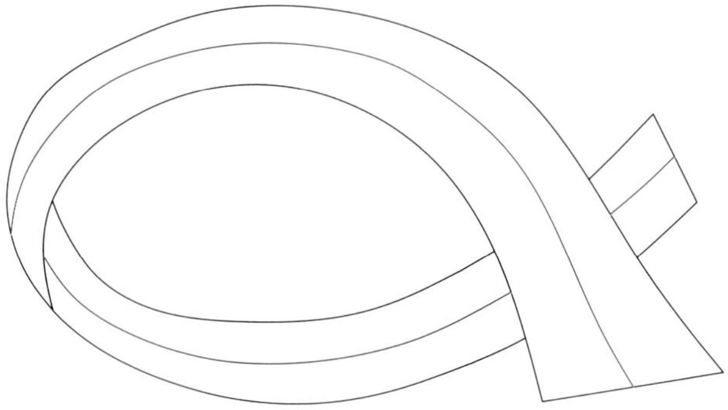

Draw centerlines.

3. Draw the brickwork grid (page 20). I used black lines on the upper half of the ribbon and blue lines on the lower half of the ribbon so that it would be easier to see the difference.

Note that as the grid approaches the flip, the brickwork size remains constant. This is because the geese do not change size or shape, but instead disappear behind the flip.

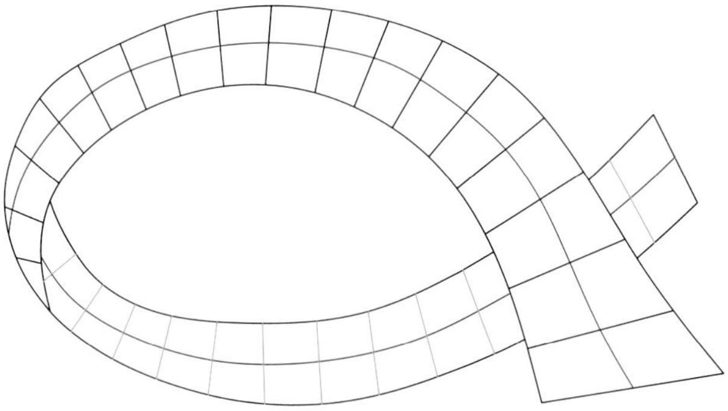

Draw brickwork.

4. Fill in with geese, beginning with the geese closest to the flip.

Notice that the geese at the point of the flip are only partial geese with their tips disappearing over the outer edge. This strengthens the illusion that this shape is folding over onto itself.

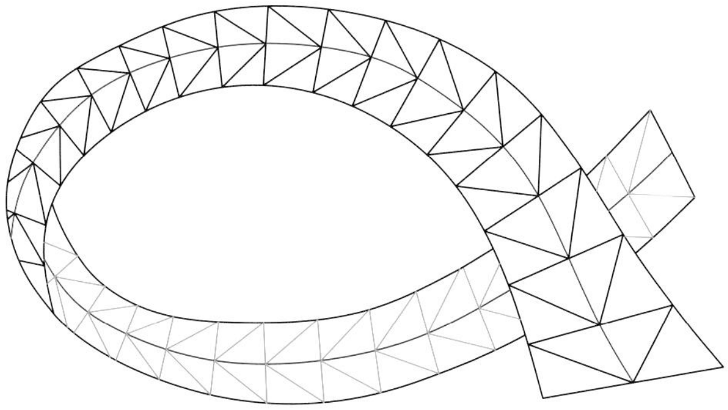

Fill in geese.

5. Erase the center dividing lines. These strips are each assembled the same as any other filler strip (see Fillers, pages 20–33).

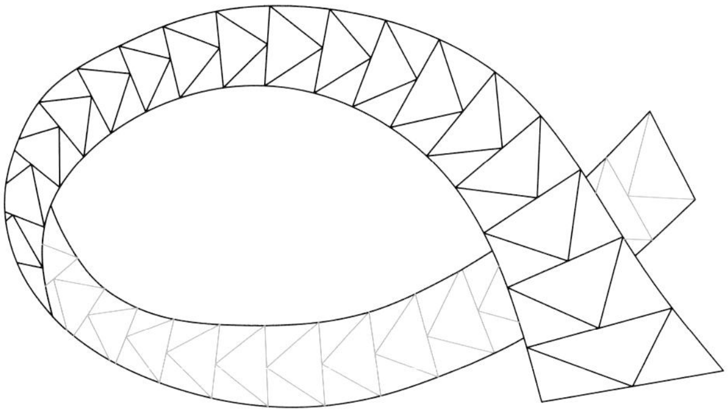

Erase centerlines.

When choosing fabrics for this illusion, the top side of the ribbon should be lighter than the underside of the ribbon. I often also make the area right beneath the flip even darker. This enhances the illusion and makes it appear as if the underside of the ribbon is in the shadow at the precise point of the flip.

Galactic Tango by Gail Garber, 2005, 39″ × 37″

Galactic Tango began its life as a classroom drawing. I wanted to see what it would look like if three rows of flying geese passed through a doughnut. Pleased with the way that design element turned out, I kept working on the design. It is one of my favorite quilts!

Detail of *Galactic Tango*

Exploding Star Points

On *Dawn of the New Day* (full quilt on page 6), I added a set of long slashing lines on the outer edge of each sky filler strip that became the rays of the sun. These lines are randomly positioned, but I am always careful to make sure they do not meet at a point on the outermost edge of the ray.

Detail of *Dawn of the New Day* (full quilt on page 6)

Driving, New Mexico Style is a dynamically rustic design that epitomizes the lifestyle in which Donna was raised, on a ranch in rural New Mexico. The only fabrics used were those she personally hand-dyed. She used the 10,000 pyramids filler with different shades and textures of hand-dyes to add subtle texture to the sunset hues of the mountains.

Driving, New Mexico Style by Donna Barnitz, 2009, 31″ × 62″

The core of the sun is a simple circular star design in the brilliant shades of orange usually seen at dusk. Its center is behind the mountains. Donna used this center to create the illusion of rays that originate from one central vanishing point. She extended lines in an outward direction until they reached the edge of the design. These straight lines form the sky filler strips, which are filled with geese. Lines are added to form the star points.

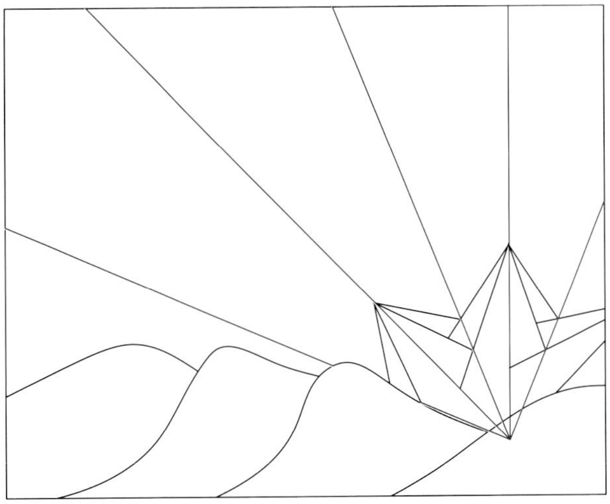

Lines drawn from vanishing point

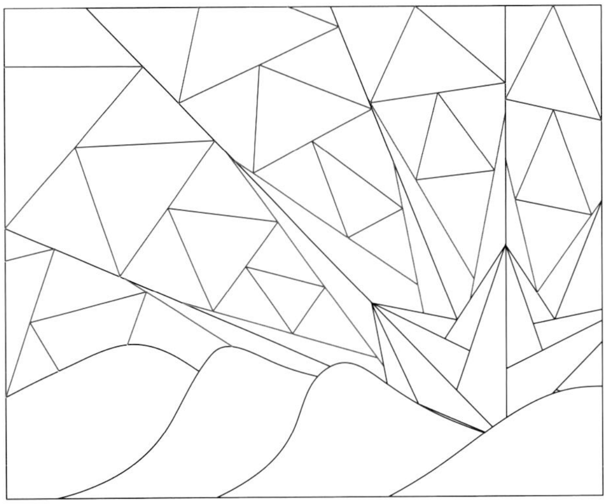

Flying geese in filler strips

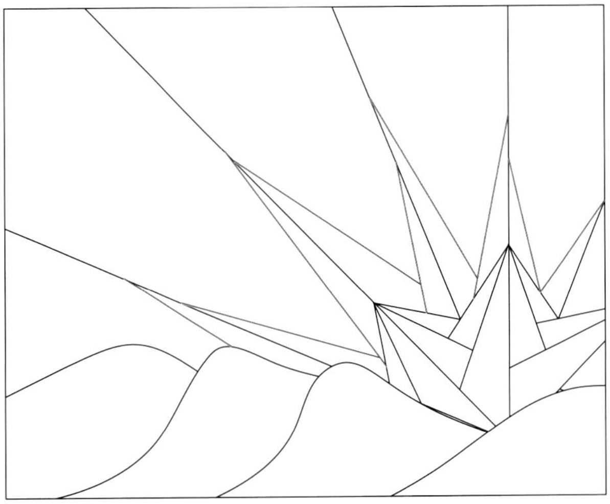

Additional lines form star points.

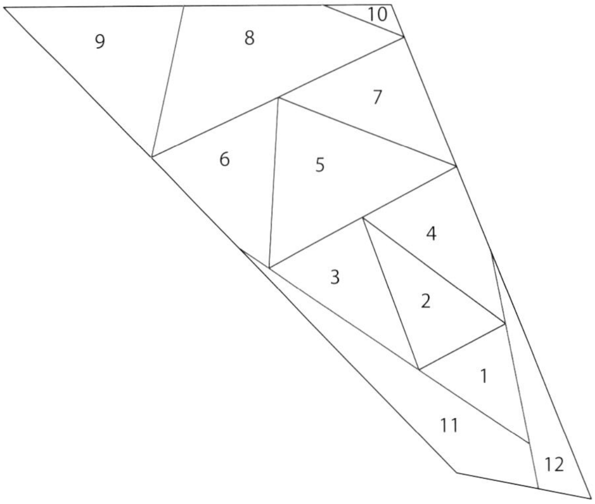

Paper-piecing order for flying geese background

The remainder of the sky was filled in with large geese in each filler strip. Notice that she carefully positioned the basic brickwork of the background sky filler strips so the points of adjacent sections were slightly offset, thereby saving herself a lot of trouble later when assembling the strips. The flying geese add texture to what otherwise might be just one piece of fabric. In order to create this effect, it is necessary to use randomly selected pastel shades of subtle solids, or prints that read as solids, for a blending effect.

This type of exploding star points is also evident in *Bernina Beyond Borders* (page 54).

These are but a few of the myriad possible design elements that can be used to create illusions in your quilts. What I love most about the use of these techniques is how they enhance all designs, from completely geometric to landscape oriented to totally whimsical.

Freezer-Paper Foundation Piecing

For many years I resisted learning to paper-foundation piece. However, as my designs became increasingly intricate, foundation piecing seemed to be the only practical way to assemble complex designs without having to make hundreds of individual templates. It wasn't long before I abandoned templates altogether and embraced my new passion for paper—freezer paper to be exact.

I began teaching this technique to my students soon afterward and was amazed at how freezer-paper foundations increased the accuracy of their stitching and the success of their designs. Foundation piecing enabled even novice sewers to successfully assemble their original designs. In this method, the fabric is positioned *beneath* the freezer-paper foundation against the bottom, waxy side of the freezer paper. It is stitched on the drawn line on the top side of the paper.

Note

With this type of foundation piecing, the finished quilt top will be a mirror image *of the original design drawing traced onto the freezer paper.*

The beauty of paper foundation piecing is that everyone, regardless of skill level, can achieve success with this technique. Each year since 1994 I have organized a fundraising quilt raffle for Hawks Aloft, the conservation organization that I co-founded. The quilt top is stitched in one weekend retreat at my mountain cabin. It appeals to both the men and the women of the group, and we generally have a good gender mix. We also attract young sewers like Lindsey Porter, age 12.

Lindsey Porter, age 12, paper-foundation pieces. *Photo by Gail Garber*

Everyone must actually work on the quilt in order to attend. Many of the novice retreat participants have never used a sewing machine, and paper-foundation piecing ensures that each block or section will fit perfectly into the overall design. At the retreat, novice sewers work on the simples blocks, while experienced stitchers assemble the parts.

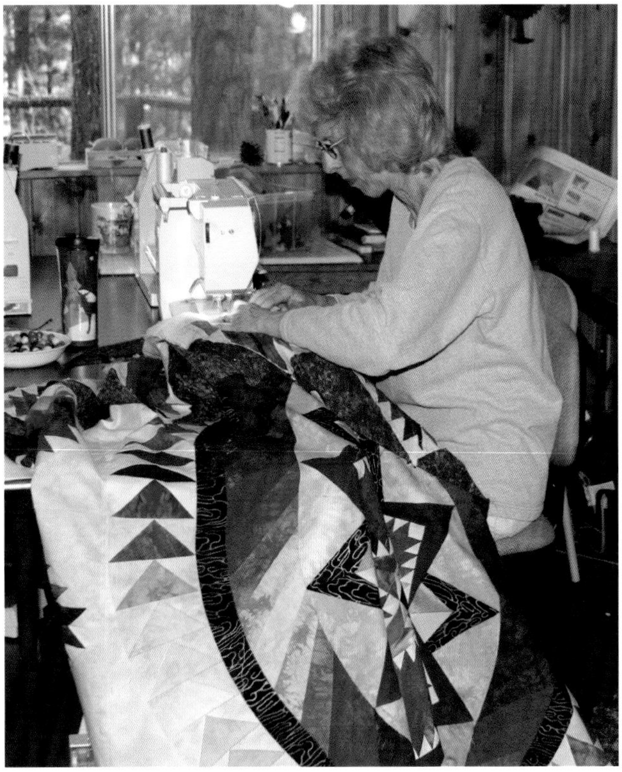

Experienced quilter Michele Hymel finishes stitching last seams on quilt. *Photo by Gail Garber*

Our 2009 quilt team of twelve finished assembling this quilt in about twelve hours. If a group of men, women, and preteens, some of whom have never before sewn, can master the technique, you can too.

Hawks Aloft Quilt Team 2009: *Standing, from L to R:* Ed Chappelle, Mary Chappelle, Mike Hymel, Michele Hymel, Anita McSorley. *Seated, from L to R:* Patty Phillips, Carolyn Sanborn, Steve Elkins, Gail Garber, Nancy Cella. *Not shown:* Ruth Burstrom, Chellye Porter, Lindsey Porter. *Photo by Steve Elkins*

I prefer freezer paper for foundations for a very practical reason. The waxy side of the freezer paper adheres to the fabric when pressed with an iron. This means that there is never more than one loose piece of fabric at a time, the piece being added at that moment. This prevents the little pleats and tucks that can be a problem with other types of foundations such as tissue paper, plain paper, and wash-away stabilizers.

Freezer paper comes in a variety of sizes, from letter-sized sheets that can be run through a standard inkjet printer to the oversized sheets necessary for large designs (available from C&T Publishing; see Resources, page 79).

Preparing the Foundation

I never cut up my final design drawing, but instead trace each freezer-paper foundation from the final design drawing, which I then call the master pattern. This ensures that there is always a backup copy in case something happens and the freezer-paper foundation is lost or destroyed.

REGISTRATION MARKS

Registration marks are the same as notches on a garment pattern. They make matching sections with opposing curves simple, and also are essential to correctly align design elements that pass beneath another portion of the design. For this exercise we will use the design *Tiny Trees*, which is included as a project beginning on page 64.

On the master pattern for the design, add registration marks about every 2″–3″ (more if a curve is sharp, and less if the shape has a relatively straight edge).

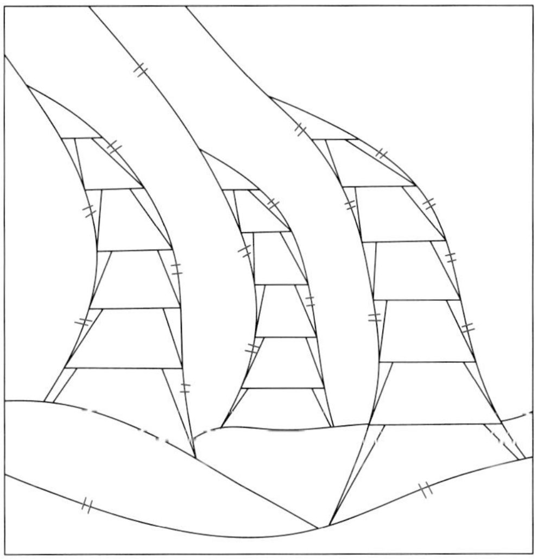

Registration marks

I use a double slash for most registration marks—these indicate simply that a matching registration mark will appear on the opposing shape.

I use three slashes to indicate the point where a seamline on the opposing piece must match an exact point on the opposing shape. The center slash indicates the exact point where the seam will meet the registration mark on the opposing piece.

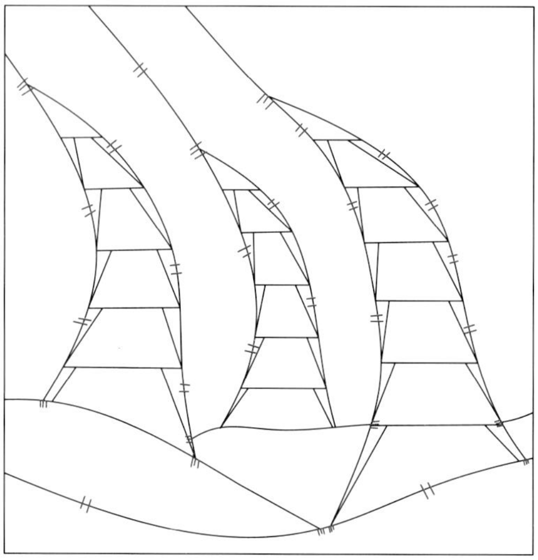

Double- and triple-slash registration marks

- For shapes that have straight edges, it may not be necessary to add registration marks.
- For shapes with sharp curves, registration marks might need to be as close as 1″–2″ apart.
- Registration marks must be added to the master pattern and then transferred to each foundation piece when it is traced.

Following these steps will ensure success later when assembling the shapes that will form your quilt.

ADDING GRAINLINES

Add a line to mark the straight of grain on all shapes that will be covered by a single piece of fabric. It is not necessary to mark the grain if one edge of the piece is a straight line and also is the outside edge of the quilt.

When a design has large sections of a single fabric, I mark the grainline on the master pattern, aligning it with the outer edge. Often, the large pieces are an irregular shape, and determining proper grainline can be difficult once the piece is separated from the master. For other pieces, mark the true vertical or horizontal grain on the master pattern. Transfer this grainline to the freezer-paper foundation. Align this grainline with either the vertical or horizontal grain of the fabric.

TRACING THE FOUNDATION

If a foundation filler strip is longer than about 12″, I often break it into smaller sections that are easier to handle.

1. Using a pencil, carefully trace all the lines on the master pattern within a particular foundation section onto the paper side of the freezer paper, being sure to also trace the registration marks from the original drawing. If necessary, number the pieces within the block or section to remind yourself of the piecing order.

2. Cut out the foundation, adding a generous seam allowance of about ¼″–½″ all the way around. This creates a visual reminder that it is necessary to leave enough fabric that extends beyond the stitching line to allow for seam allowances.

Use the same method above to prepare a freezer-paper foundation for shapes that will be covered by a single piece of fabric. Transfer the grainlines marked on the master pattern to the foundation. This foundation will be ironed to the wrong side of a single piece of fabric and then cut out.

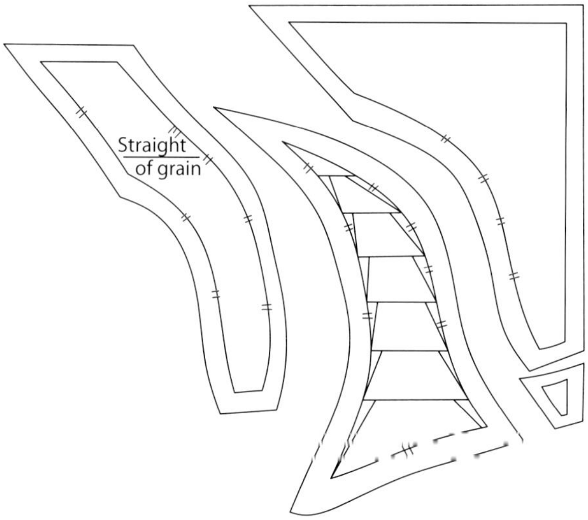

Cut out foundations.

MAKING MULTIPLE FOUNDATIONS OF THE SAME PIECE

For some designs it is necessary to make multiple copies of the same foundation, such as with a block repeat pattern or a symmetrical circular star or repetitive border design. When this happens, create a master foundation for each design area by tracing each line within each individual foundation onto a sheet of freezer paper, and then adding the outer seam allowances. Cut enough additional pieces of freezer paper, one for each needed repeat unit, that are large enough to contain the master foundation.

If the design requires that all the foundations be exactly alike, stack 4 sheets of the cut freezer paper at a time with the waxy side facing up and the master foundation on top with the paper side facing down.

Bring the entire stack to your sewing machine and stitch without thread, following all the lines on the master foundation. Use a 14/90 size needle and set your stitch length to 2.5mm.

This will automatically create duplicate copies of the pattern, so that all the stitched images look exactly like the drawing in the master pattern. These finished pieces will *not* be a mirror image of the master design. That was corrected when making the additional foundation.

If the design requires that half of the blocks be a mirror image, that is, some foundations are the exact opposite of the original, then place half of the freezer-paper sheets waxy side down and half of the sheets waxy side up, with the master foundation placed as before. This will automatically give you the mirror-image blocks.

I stack only 4 sheets of freezer paper at a time so as to reduce wear and tear on my sewing machine needle and to prevent slippage.

Measuring and Cutting

Two common methods used for cutting fabrics prior to piecing are to "cut a hunk" (or "whack a chunk") and to precut fabrics to the appropriate size for each section. I prefer the latter because it actually is faster in the long run, and some pieces can be measured and cut so the grainline falls along the outside edge of the piece, thereby minimizing stretch. However, I use the cut-a-hunk method when I am working with a fabric that is hand-painted or a series of hand-dyed gradations that must be kept strictly in order for that particular design.

CUT A HUNK

With the cut-a-hunk method, you pick up the fabric to be used, look at the space it needs to cover, and then whack out a chunk that looks about right. The drawbacks to this method are that your fabric piece might not be large enough to adequately cover the necessary space, and the grainline may not be in the best position for the finished quilt.

PRECUT TO SIZE

My general rule for measuring is to *add at least 1″ to the length and width of the piece that needs to be covered.* When working with a filler strip in which many pieces will be nearly the same size, such as this strip of a tiny tree, measure the length and width of the largest piece and precut the correct number of pieces.

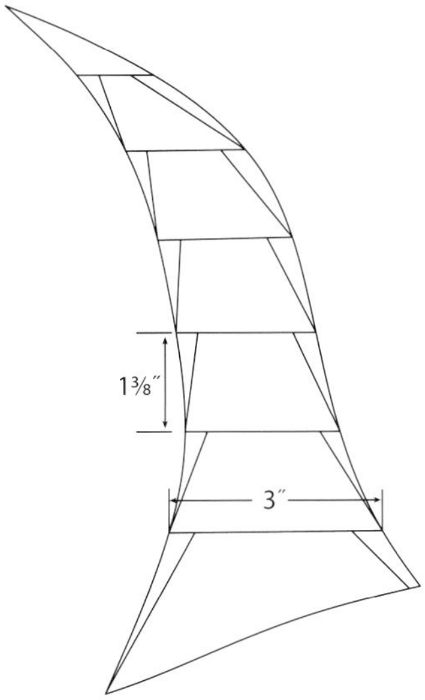

Measure length and width.

Here, the exact measurements are 3″ × 1⅜″. Round up small fractions to the easiest cutting size. For this strip, cut 6 pieces of tree fabric that measure 4″ × 2½″ because there are 6 pieces of tree that generally fit this shape.

When one piece is quite a bit larger than the other pieces, such as the bottommost piece of the tree, measure and cut that piece separately.

Sometimes a foundation has several long, narrow pieces, such as the background in *Tiny Trees.*

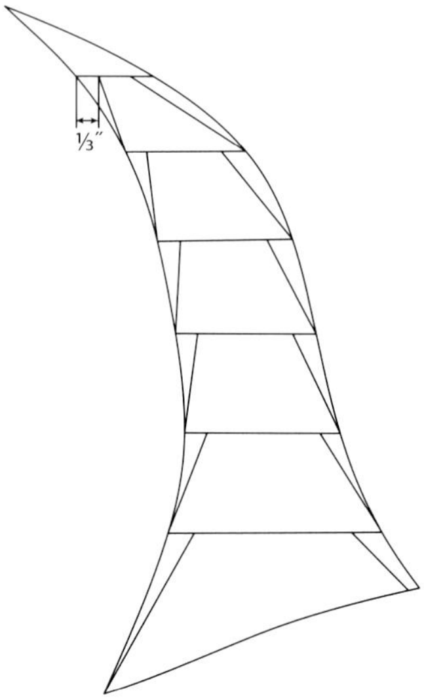

Narrow pieces

This strip of background fabric is about ⅓″ wide. Cut a strip of fabric on the crosswise grain that is 1½″ wide, which is enough to cover the widest piece. Once the strip is stitched in place, trim off the excess.

CUTTING THE GOOSE PIECES

In the case of a strip of flying geese, measure the largest goose in that section and cut all the pieces the same size unless there is a dramatic change in the size of the geese within that strip.

The largest goose (below) measures about 2½″ × 1¼″, but the smaller geese in the section at the far end of the strip measure about 1¾″ × 1″. Add 1″ to each of these measurements. Cut the geese for this strip in 2 separate batches, 6 pieces 3½″ × 2¼″ and 8 pieces 2¾″ × 2″, for a total of 14 geese.

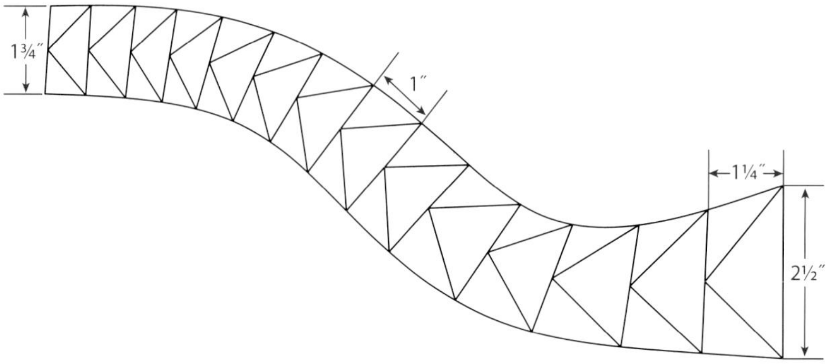

Measure largest and smallest goose in section and add 1″ to length and width.

For the background pieces, measure the longest edge of the largest background piece. The 2 longest sides measure about 1¼″ long. Add 2″ to this measurement. Cut 14 squares 3¼″ × 3¼″, and cut them in half diagonally.

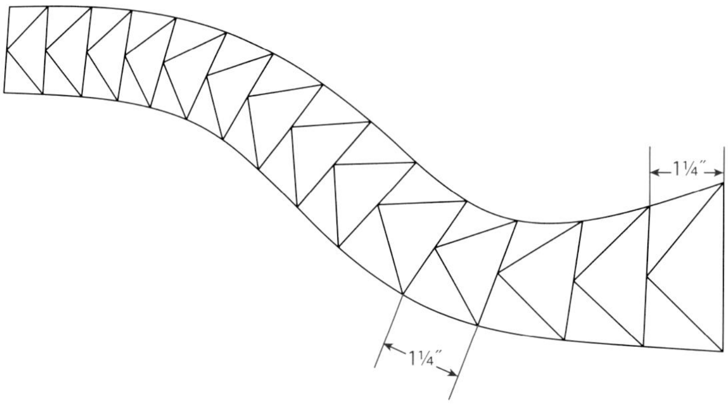

Measure largest background piece and add 2″.

This will create both background pieces, and the straight of grain will generally lie along the outside edge, helping to minimize stretch.

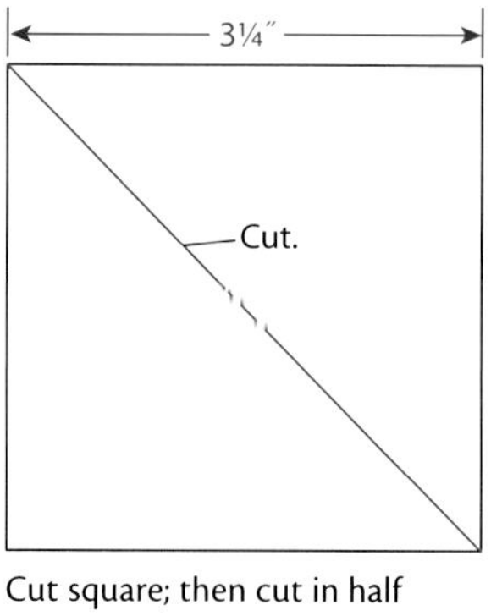

Cut square; then cut in half diagonally.

Stitching the Strips

There are a variety of different styles when it comes to paper-foundation piecing. This style, with the paper placed on top of the fabric, can be confusing, especially for novices. Carol Doak has revolutionized paper-foundation piecing by developing proven methods that are easy to understand, even for beginners, and I've found her techniques to be superior in the classroom. The directions below are very similar to those that Carol uses in her foundation-piecing classes.

Set the stitch length on your sewing machine to 1.5mm for foundation piecing. This will help perforate the paper for easier removal and help reduce popped stitches when removing the paper. Refer to the fillers chapter (pages 20–33) for numbering the piecing order of the different types of strips.

1. Begin by positioning the wrong side of fabric piece 1 to the waxy side of the freezer paper. Press this in place.

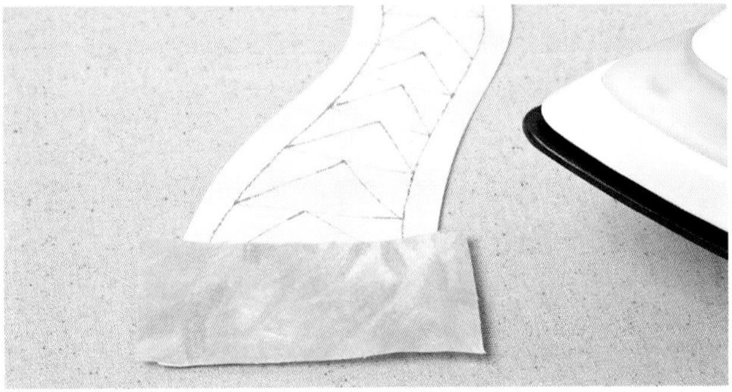

Position wrong side of fabric on waxy side of freezer paper. Press.

2. Place the strip, fabric side down, on a cutting mat.

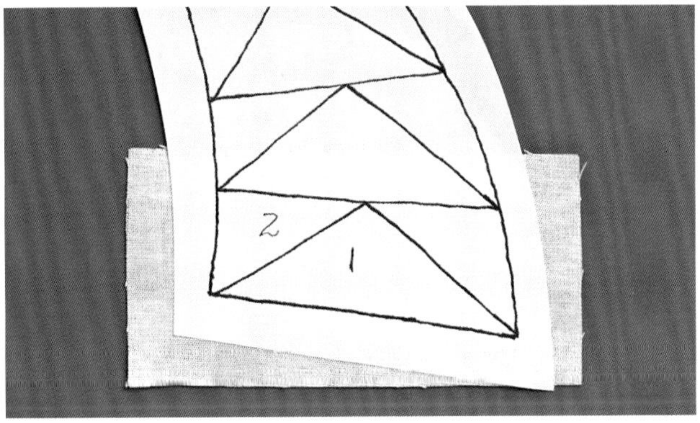

Place fabric side down.

3. Align a thin piece of cardboard, such as the edge of a postcard, with the line that separates pieces 1 and 2.

Align edge of card.

4. Fold the paper over the edge of the card, position the ¼″ mark of your ruler over this edge, and trim the excess fabric so all that remains is the ¼″ seam allowance.

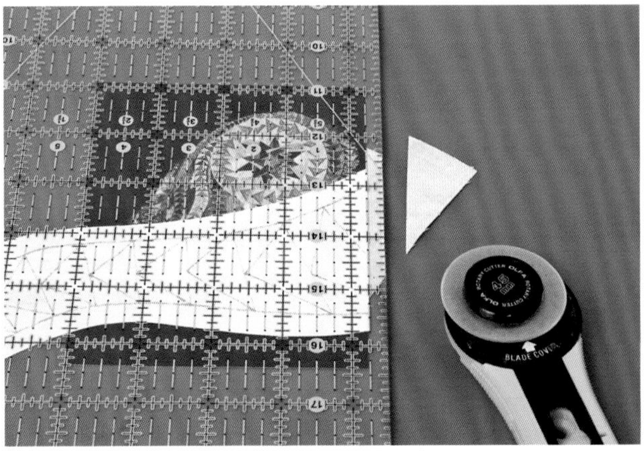

Fold paper over card and trim to ¼″ seam allowance.

5. Repeat the trimming with the other side of the first goose.

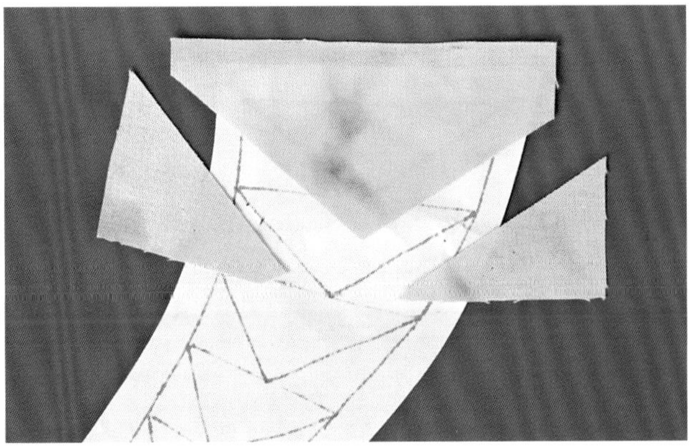

Trim other side to ¼″ seam allowance.

6. Align fabric piece 2 to the raw edge that has just been trimmed, placing the fabrics right sides together.

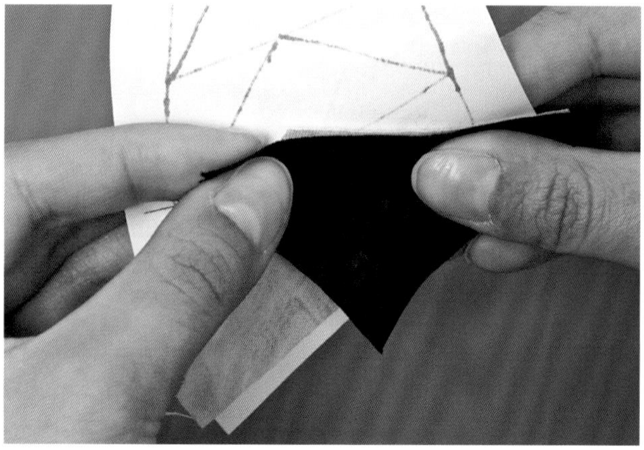

Align fabric piece 2.

7. Turn the foundation over so the paper is on top. Stitch along the seamline between pieces 1 and 2, stitching a couple of stitches beyond the end of the piece.

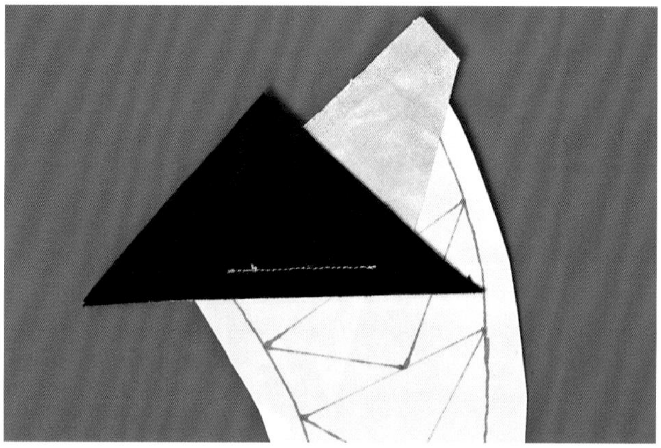

Stitch seamline. Photo shows view from back after stitching is complete.

8. Press this piece in place.

Press.

To press, lightly finger-press the piece, and then lightly press it on the fabric side of the section, being careful not to touch the iron to the waxy side of the freezer paper. Then, turn the foundation over and press securely on the paper side of the foundation. This will securely hold the fabric in position.

9. Repeat with the background piece on the opposite side of the goose.

Stitch and press other side of goose.

10. Once both backgrounds have been pressed, repeat Steps 2–4 above, folding the paper foundation back over the edge of a postcard and trimming the raw edges to a ¼″ seam allowance.

Trim to ¼″ seam allowances.

11. Align the second goose with the trimmed edges. Stitch in place.

Align second goose.

12. Fold back and press.

13. Continue working in this fashion until the entire strip is covered with fabric.

14. Trim the seam allowances around the entire piece to ¼″.

Flying geese strip

Trimming Irregular Edges: A Great Trick

This is my favorite way to add the ¼″ seam allowance to the edge of an irregularly shaped piece.

1. Align the ¼″ line of a 4″ square ruler with the drawn stitching line on the paper side of the foundation. Place the rotary cutting blade alongside the edge of the ruler, and "drive" the ruler and cutter in tandem along the edge of the foundation.

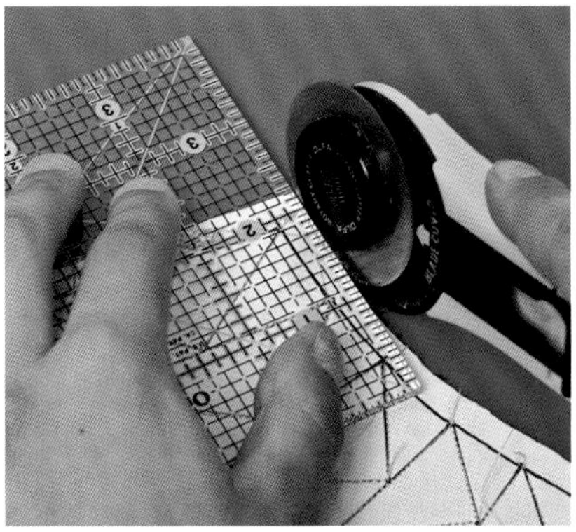

"Drive" ruler and cutter to add ¼″ seam allowance.

Focus on the space about midpoint on the ruler so the cutting blade remains about in the center of the ruler. It works like magic, but you must concentrate.

2. After each paper-foundation section is trimmed, transfer the registration marks to the wrong side of the fabric, marking within the seam allowances. Lay the shape back onto the master pattern to check to see if all registration marks have been transferred.

3. Remove the paper. The foundation paper must be removed prior to stitching curved sections together. If the sections to be joined are straight edges, then removing the paper is optional.

I have found that if you apply a bit of tension to the filler strip, the freezer paper will loosen, making it easier to remove.

Assembling the Sections: Piecing

All seam allowances are ¼″ when assembling these designs.

Assembling the individual shapes into a finished quilt top can be a lot like putting together a jigsaw puzzle, depending on the complexity of the design. Because the finished quilt is a mirror image of the master pattern, properly positioning the shapes can be confusing. For this reason, I like to lay my trimmed pieces onto the master pattern, paper side up, so I can check positioning relative to the other shapes.

Assemble the background first and work toward the foreground.

1. Number each unit on the master pattern and also transfer that number to each foundation.

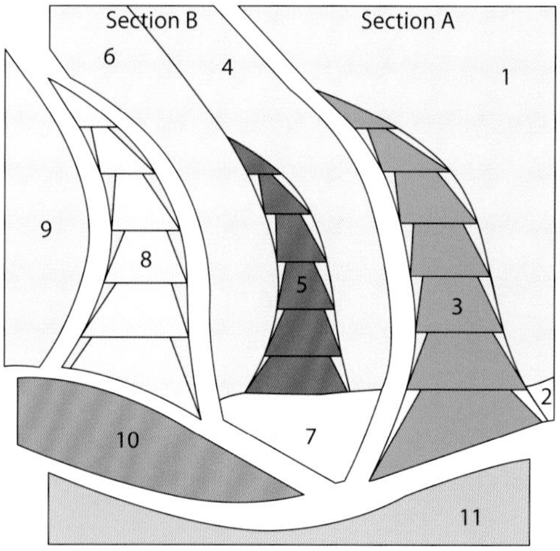

Number each unit.

Notice that some of the units must first be assembled into sections before other units can be attached.

2. Pin the shapes together at each registration mark, right sides together, and then place additional pins in between if necessary, particularly on sharp curves.

I use lots of pins when piecing curves. My philosophy is that I would rather pin more and rip out less.

3. Stitch with a ¼″ seam allowance. Use a standard stitch length of 2–2.5mm when stitching without paper foundations.

4. Press the seams toward the side of least resistance, generally away from a heavily pieced filler strip.

5. Continue adding shapes until the entire quilt top is complete.

When stitching curves, I generally place the piece with the outer curve on top. However, if I am joining a foundation-pieced section to another that is a solid piece of fabric, I almost always place the foundation-pieced section on top. By doing so, I can see where to stitch to ensure that all my points will be perfect.

Flat Piping

This method works well when using a filler strip as an accent for another design, such as a garment, purse, or pocket edge, or just as a simpler way to apply a few filler strips. Although simple, it does have some drawbacks, such as extra bulk at the edges of a filler strip that can blunt the sharp points within the strip.

1. Cut a bias strip of fabric 1″ wide and as long as both sides of the filler strip. Press in half lengthwise, with wrong sides together.

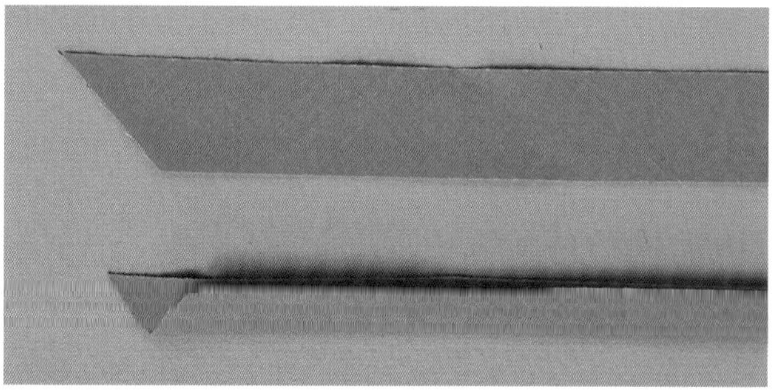

Cut strip to length and press in half lengthwise.

This will create a flat piping strip ½″ wide with the right side out on both sides.

2. Matching raw edges, stitch the flat piping to one edge of the filler strip.

Stitch piping to edge.

3. Repeat to attach the flat piping to the other edge of the filler strip.

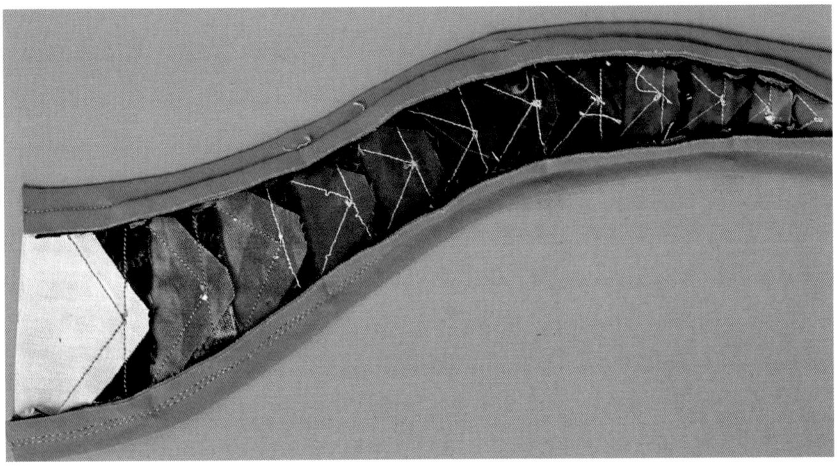

Turn seam allowances under.

4. Turn the seam allowances under and press firmly, leaving the piping extending beyond the edge of the filler strip.

5. Pin the strip in place on the fabric.

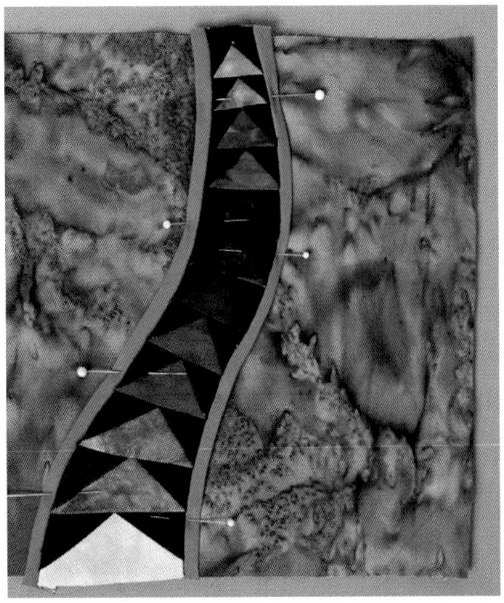

Pin.

6. Stitch in-the-ditch of the piping, using matching thread.

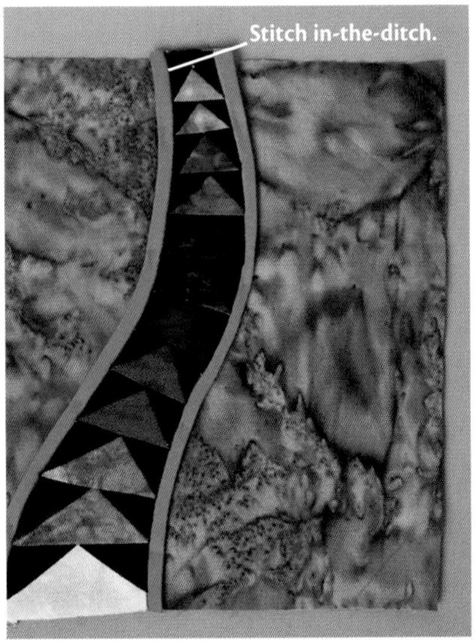

Stitch in-the-ditch of the piping.

Finishing

Using your favorite basic quilting book or using the online C&T Publishing Quiltmaking Basics (Tips and Techniques, page 80), add borders and layer the quilt with batting and backing. Baste and quilt as desired. Add binding and a sleeve.

Gallery Quilts

Bernina Beyond Borders by Gail Garber, 2008, 44″ × 32″
Collection of Bernina of America

This quilt was inspired by my Bernina National Artisan's trip to Switzerland to visit the headquarters of Bernina; tour the factory; and learn more about the company's history, its strict standards of quality, and the philosophy that drives the family-owned-and-operated company.

Sailing Away by Gail Garber, 2009, 14" circle

The thought of sailing away to some exotic island just makes me want to get busy planning for a monthlong sojourn to a land without time, cell phones, and television. Your fantasy destination might be different, but just as wonderful. This little quilt is a snap to make—a perfect gift for a friend who loves to travel or wishes that she could. For those of us who live far from the ocean, the very idea of traveling by sailboat evokes the romance of the high seas.

Sylvia—A Life's Journey by Gail Garber, 2006, 34" × 30"

This quilt was made for the Alzheimer's Art Quilt Initiative to raise awareness and funds to help find a cure for this disease. The image is of my mom, done from a photo taken on her wedding day—a day when we all believe that life will be rosy, as reflected by the bright colors of the first section. The second section represents the years after having six children, when there were a few bumps in the road. The final section, which is dark and stormy, represent the years after my father's death, with Mom locked in the grip of dementia. The red slashes represent my joy at being able to be near her in these final years, and through it all, she is surrounded with love by her six children. The flying geese in this section are in our birth order—girl, boy, boy, girl, girl, boy.

Photo by Lee Kirchner, Axis Creative Group, Troy, Michigan

Olivia Octopus by Marsha Cardwell, 2008, 22¼″ × 28½″

The challenge that I gave myself while designing this quilt was to find an element in nature that had natural twists and curves that would lend themselves to curved flying geese. An octopus popped into my head. I had a fat quarter of a Kaffe Fassett circular print that would give the illusion of the round suction pads on the tentacles. I used a layered effect in the quilt, starting with the top representing the sandy beach, and then added blue, from light to deep dark, to give the illusion that Olivia was down deep in the ocean.

Raven Lets Loose the Light
by Mary Cadman, 2006, 26″ × 36″

According to some First Nations legends, the raven stole the sun and brought light to the people. With that legend as inspiration, my quilt lets Raven bring the northern lights.

Raven Lets Loose the Light grew out of a guild challenge—design something that flies, with no more than two straight edges on the quilt. I have always been fond of ravens, so the "something that flies" was an easy choice. While doodling with the design using the spiral flying geese, the idea of a ball of northern lights being unwound by Raven occurred to me.

The background quilting also represents the northern lights. I raided my father-in-law's fly-tying desk for the feathers on the bottom and my husband's bird-carving supplies for the eye.

On Golden Pond by Michele Hymel, 2009, 47″ × 41″

This quilt was inspired by my love of the vivid colors and vibrant textures of nature, especially aquatic life. I don't aim for a literal representation, but rather an evocation of the shapes, movements, colors, and designs found in the natural world. Quilting is my passion and my method of creative and artistic expression.

Portrait of Elegance by Anita McSorley, 2009, 34″ × 46″

Coming across a sketch I made many years ago of a lady wearing a large, broad-brimmed hat, I recognized the possibility of incorporating patches of flying geese within the folds of her garment and wrap. The brim of the hat was the perfect place to design a paper-pieced mountains and valleys border. The curvilinear background completes the look I wanted to finish the piece.

My Geese Garden by Sue Soetenga, 2009, 21″ × 24″

I find curved geese designs absolutely fascinating. I was originally hoping to create a quilt with imaginary flowers. The result was a piece that reminds me of gardens that bloom during the long, hot summers of east Texas. My greatest joy as a quilter was to discover that small and numerous patches that fit together perfectly are actually possible.

Playing with Geese by Pam Ventgen, 2009, 48″ × 26″

I've done all types of traditional piecing for years, but Gail's class provided the opportunity and challenge (with her guidance) of designing my own pattern and learning how to include elements of free-form flying geese and unique background shapes. Once I got started, it was exciting to see it evolve into a completed quilt.

Fireworks over Sydney by Sandra Long, 2009, 46″ × 50″

I went through Gail's previous book and immediately saw fireworks, and what better way to display them but above the Harbour Bridge in Sydney, Australia. My artistic background led me to design a too-detailed picture, with thousands of pieces. But as I progressed with my design, I took artistic license to downplay the detail. As the quilt progressed it seemed too dark, and then I totally stepped out of my box and discovered color. What fun I had putting colors and textures together. Then came the embellishment and discovery of new media. What a journey!

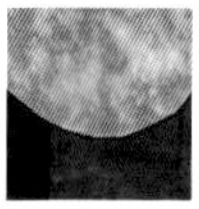

Egyptian Twilight by Lisa Stewart, 2009, 24″ × 37″

The quilt design was inspired by Gail's ideas on how to offset the flying geese pattern. I have always wanted to go to Egypt and had just finished reading about Antony and Cleopatra, so I had the images of the great pyramids in mind.

Mums the Word by Cathy Combs, 2009, 30″ × 27″

My quilt evolved from the chrysanthemum. It is a flower that appears to grow in a multifaceted way from the center to the flower's edge. I decided to alter my original design by incorporating several of the design techniques learned in classes taken from Gail.

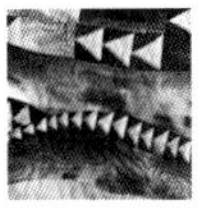

Night Flight over Water by Mary Chappelle, 2009, 42″ × 34″

This quilt was inspired when I stopped to look over a valley, and through my binoculars I saw streams of migrating cranes that were not visible to the naked eye. I changed the real-life vision to one of geese over the moon, when I learned that geese migrate at night. The quilt combines machine piecing with appliqué and paint embellishments and is machine quilted.

Punda Milia by Patricia Drennan, 2009, 50″ × 42½″

I have used random curved flying geese in many of my quilts depicting birds, flowers, and even a tiger. The geese lend themselves especially well to striped animals. The challenge with *Punda Milia* (Swahili for "zebra") was to construct the entire animal out of alternating black and white flying geese stripes. I arranged the stripes so the white ones ran in the opposite direction from the black ones and used many different fabrics, so the zebra also has a delightful scrappy effect. Here and there, I placed a stripe of simple triangles and solid pieces to add interest. *Punda Milia* is paper pieced, hand appliquéd, and machine quilted.

Song of the Lyrebird by Patricia Drennan, 2006, 31½″ × 32″

The original intent of this design was to depict some kind of bird with a magnificent display of tail feathers. The obvious choice would have been a peacock, but I wanted something a little different, so I started researching photos of the lyrebird. This piece is a compilation of that study. The tail feathers are paper pieced; most of the rest of the quilt is hand appliquéd. It is machine quilted and embellished with couched decorative yarns.

What Do Fish Have to Do with It?
by Polly Sepulvado, 2008, 63″ × 74″

I buy a fabric I love (sometimes too much and sometimes too little, which causes a creativity stretch) and make rather traditional blocks. This design took on a life of its own and grew into what you see here. I took photographs of the blocks in different arrangements to determine which one was the most pleasing. All of my quilts have graced the walls of my medical office at one time or another.

Mixed Emotions by Mary Chappelle, 2006, 36″ × 32″

This quilt started as random drawing, and then I added different fillers—geese and variations. I actually ended up sewing it at a time of high stress in my life, including caring for an aging and ill mother, and thus the title.

Star Fragments

Finished quilt size: 32½″ × 24½″

Block size: 14″ × 10″ finished

Star Fragments, simplified two-block design adaptation by Gail Garber and Michele Hymel, 2009

Bright and sassy, this beautiful scrap quilt was designed and sewn in just one day by Julie May of Harlingen, Texas. Julie's original design featured four different rectangular blocks with a radiating star that extends into the border.

You'll make two A blocks and two B blocks, each measuring 14″ × 10″ (finished), all pieced on foundation papers. Two blocks are rotated to complete the center star. Chose to buy yardage or make it scrappy!

Julie May's original design, 2009, 36″ × 30″

Design

Materials

Tan background: 1½ yards

Green geese: ⅔ yard total

Lime green accent: ¼ yard

Light red center star: ⅛ yard

Dark red center star and points: ¼ yard

Gold/yellow star: ¼ yard total

Red/orange star: ¼ yard total

Dark blue star: ⅛ yard

Light blue star: ⅛ yard

Dark purple star: ⅛ yard

Light purple star: ⅛ yard

Purple inner border: ¼ yard

Purple outer border: ⅓ yard

Backing: ⅞ yard

Batting: 35″ × 27″

Binding: ⅓ yard

Sleeve: ⅜ yard

Cutting

Strips are cut cross-grain (selvage to selvage). A 40″ width of fabric is assumed. Foundation patterns are on pullout pages P3 and P4. For this project, cut pieces are sized generously to enable quicker precutting and for ease in aligning the narrow angles of the shapes.

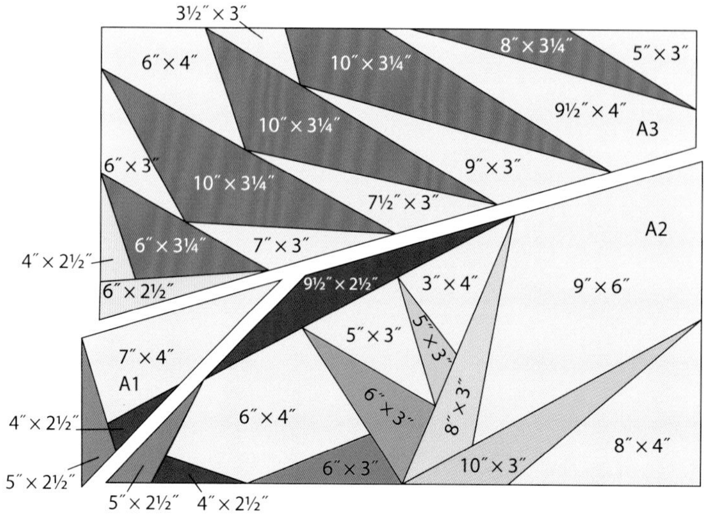

Block A with fabric cutting sizes

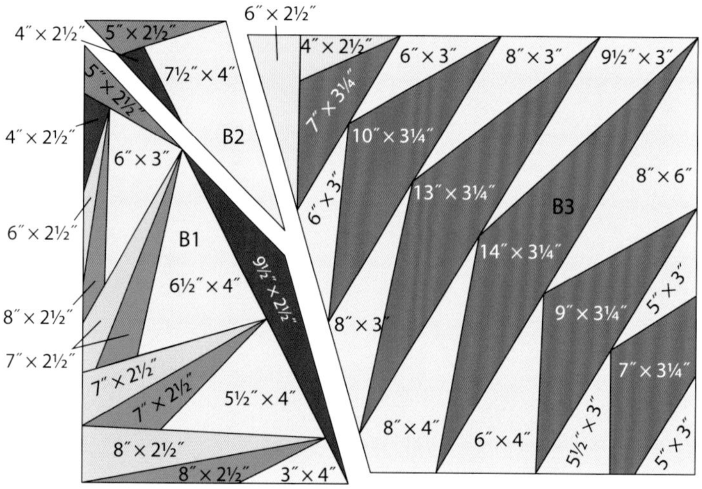

Block B with fabric cutting sizes

Tan background:

Cut 6 strips 3″ wide. Subcut as directed in cutting diagrams.

Cut 4 strips 4″ wide. Subcut as directed in cutting diagrams.

Cut 2 rectangles 9″ × 6″ for piece 10 in foundation A2 (see pullout page P3).

Cut 2 rectangles 8″ × 6″ for piece 7 in foundation B3 (see pullout page P4).

Green geese:

Cut 6 strips 3¼″ wide. Subcut as directed in cutting diagrams.

Lime green accent:
Cut 2 strips 2½″ wide. Subcut into 4 rectangles 6″ × 2½″ and 4 rectangles 4″ × 2½″.

Light red center star:
Cut 1 strip 2½″ wide. Subcut into 8 rectangles 5″ × 2½″.

Dark red center star and points:
Cut 2 strips 2½″ wide. Subcut into 8 rectangles 4″ × 2½″ and 4 rectangles 9½″ × 2½″.

Gold/yellow star:
Cut 3″ strips of your chosen fabrics. Subcut as directed in cutting diagrams.

Red/orange star:
Cut 3″ strips of your chosen fabrics. Subcut as directed in cutting diagrams.

Dark blue and light blue star:
Cut 1 strip 2½″ wide of each. Subcut as directed in cutting diagrams.

Dark purple and light purple star:
Cut 1 strip 2½″ wide of each. Subcut as directed in cutting diagrams.

Purple inner border:
Cut 4 strips 1″ wide.

Purple outer border:
Cut 4 strips 2″ wide.

Binding:
Cut 4 strips 2¼″ wide.

Sleeve:
Cut 1 rectangle 32″ × 8½″.

Foundations

Make 2 freezer-paper foundations (page 45) for each of the following pieces: A1, A2, A3, B1, B2, and B3.

Construction

1. As shown in the Assembly Diagram (below), one of the block A stars will be gold/yellow and the other will be red/orange. Following the method described in Stitching the Strips (pages 49–52), paper piece all 6 A1, A2, and A3 foundations. Then, stitch an A1 to an A2 and press. Add A3 and press. Repeat to make the second A block. Trim the outside seam allowances to ¼″.

2. Similarly, one of the block B stars will be light and dark purple and the other will be light and dark blue. As in Step 1, paper piece all 6 B1, B2, and B3 foundations. Then, stitch a B1 to a B2 and press. Add B3 and press. Repeat to make the second B block. Trim the outside seam allowances to ¼″.

3. Join an A block and a B block together along their long lengths as shown. Press. Repeat for the second pair of A and B blocks.

4. Rotate 1 A/B unit 180°. Join the 2 A/B units together along the center seam to complete the center of the quilt so that the central star emerges, as shown. Press. Remove the paper.

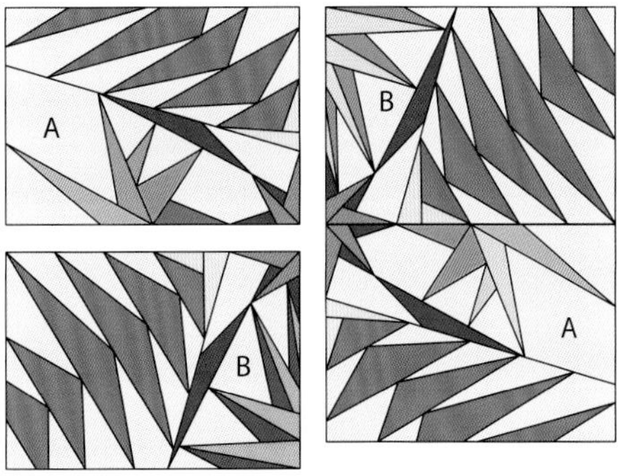

Assembly Diagram

ADD THE BORDERS

1. Stitch the inner border strips to the outer border strips. Press the seams to one side. There is extra length for mitering and trimming.

2. Center each border on the quilt. Stitch, leaving ¼″ at each end unstitched, and backstitch at each end.

3. Fold the quilt diagonally, so a pair of adjacent borders is aligned. Mark a 45° miter line using a ruler. Stitch on the line, backstitching at each end. Trim to a ¼″ seam allowance. Press the seam open. Repeat at the remaining corners. For further information on this process, see C&T Quiltmaking Basics (Tips and Techniques, page 80).

Finishing

Your quilt top is complete. Layer the quilt top, batting, and backing; baste and quilt as desired; and bind (page 53). Add a sleeve and a label to your quilt.

Tiny Trees

Finished quilt size: 15½″ × 15½″

Tiny Trees by Gail Garber and Donna Barnitz, 2009

Tiny trees, blowing in the wind, are a whimsical variation of the flying geese filler. This fun project can be easily stitched in just one day. The project includes a 12-inch finished block, stitched with paper foundations, as well as prairie points with button embellishments.

Design

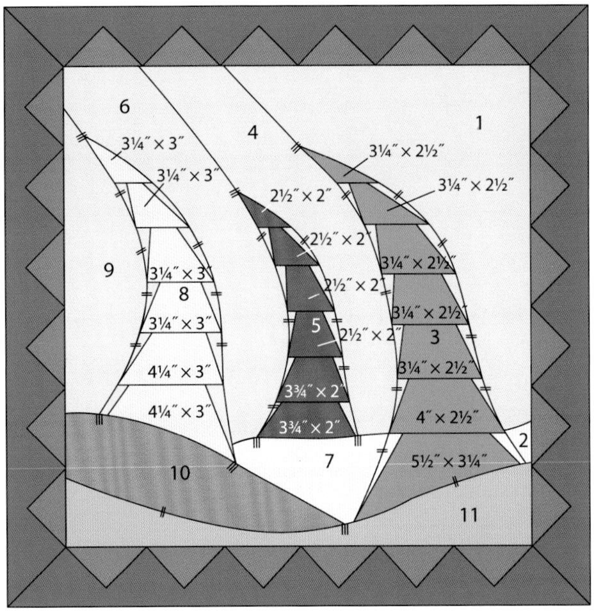

Cutting diagram with piece sizes

Materials

Blue sky: ½ yard

Green trees: Fat eighth each of 3 different fabrics

Green landscape: ⅛ yard each of 3 different prints

Red prairie points: ¼ yard total of assorted prints

Blue border: ¼ yard

Backing: 18″ × 18″

Batting: 18″ × 18″

Binding: ¼ yard

24 buttons: ¼″ diameter

Sleeve: ⅜ yard

Cutting

Strips are cut cross-grain (selvage to selvage). A 40″ width of fabric is assumed. The template and foundation patterns for this project are on pullout page P1.

Blue sky:
Trace template patterns 1, 4, 6, and 9 (pattern pullout page P1) onto freezer paper. Press onto the *wrong* side of the fabric and cut out. Be sure to align the vertical or horizontal fabric grain with either the outer straight edge of the block or the grainlines shown on the template. Transfer the registration marks to the wrong side of the fabric on these pieces before removing the paper.

Blue sky (tree background):
Cut 3 strips 1½″ wide. Subcut into 30 rectangles 3¼″ × 1½″.

Green tree 3 (left):
Cut 1 rectangle 5½″ × 3¼″.

Cut 1 rectangle 4″ × 2½″.

Cut 5 rectangles 3¼″ × 2½″.

Green tree 5 (center):
Cut 2 rectangles 3¾″ × 2″.

Cut 4 rectangles 2½″ × 2″.

Green tree 8 (right):
Cut 2 rectangles 4¼″ × 3″.

Cut 4 rectangles 3¼″ × 3″.

Green landscape:
Trace template patterns 2, 7, 10, and 11 (pattern pullout page P1) onto freezer paper. Follow the directions for blue sky (above) to cut out these green landscape fabric pieces. Cut 1 rectangle 1½″ × 4″ and 1 rectangle 1½″ × 3″ for foundation piecing the green segments 2 and 3 on the sides of the base of tree 3 (left).

Red prairie points:
Cut 24 squares 2½″ × 2½″.

Blue border:
Cut 4 rectangles 2″ × 20″.

Binding:
Cut 2 strips 2¼″ wide.

Sleeve:
Cut 1 strip 15″ × 8½″.

Foundations

Make 1 freezer-paper foundation (page 45) for each of the following tree pieces: 3, 5, and 8.

Construction

1. Following the method described in Stitching the Strips (pages 49–52), paper piece the trees. Follow the piecing order on the foundation pattern. Trim the outside seam allowances to ¼″. Transfer the registration marks to the wrong side of the fabric. Remove the paper.

2. This design must be assembled in sections. Note that section A contains pieces 1, 2, and 3. Stitch 1 to 2, press, and then stitch these to 3 and press. This completes section A.

3. Section B consists of pieces 4, 5, 6, and 7. Stitch 4 to 5, press, and then stitch these to 6 and press. Stitch these to 7 and press.

4. Stitch section A to section B and press.

5. When these 2 sections are assembled, the remaining pieces are added in order: 8, 9, 10, and 11.

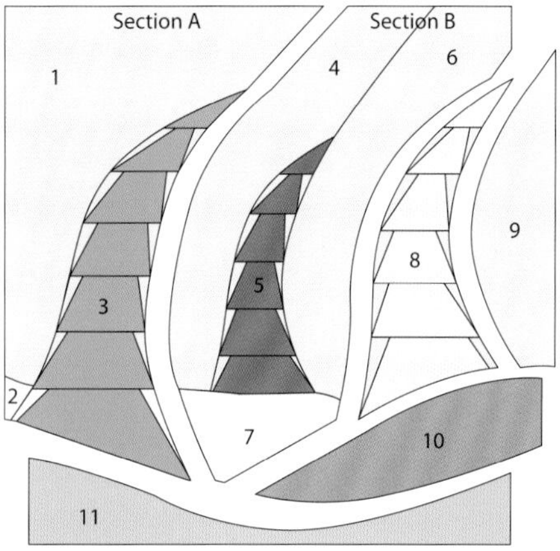

Assembly Diagram

ADDING PRAIRIE POINTS

1. Fold each square in half so that it forms a rectangle that measures 1¼″ × 2½″. Fold both corners in to the center to form the prairie point with a fold down the middle. Press.

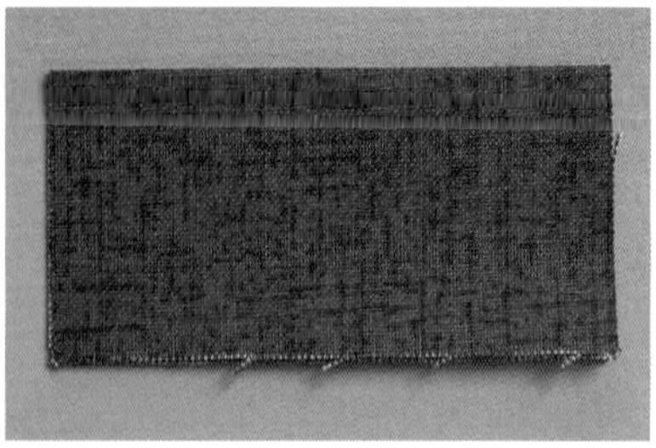
Fold in half.

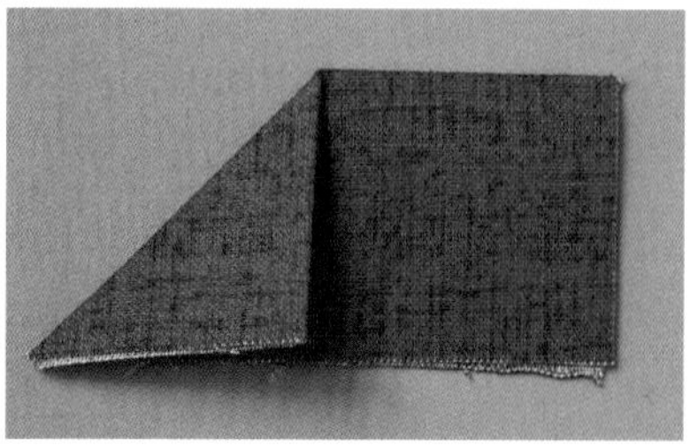
Fold corner down.

Fold second corner down.

2. Position 6 prairie points on each side of the quilt top, overlapping the side corners as necessary to fit evenly. The center folds of the prairie points face the right side of the quilt top and they point toward the quilt top center. Stitch these in place with a scant ¼″ seam allowance.

ADDING OUTER BORDER

1. Center each border piece over the quilt top edge and the prairie points. Pin in place. Place the machine needle about ½″ in from the block corner. Backstitch to ¼″ from the edge of the block, and then stitch forward until reaching ¼″ from the other end of the block. Backstitch to hold the border in place. Repeat on the remaining sides.

2. Fold the quilt diagonally, so 2 adjacent borders are aligned. Mark a 45° miter line using a ruler. Stitch on the line, backstitching at each end. Trim to a ¼″ seam allowance. Press the seam open. Repeat 3 more times at the remaining corners. For further information on this process, see C&T Quiltmaking Basics (Tips and Techniques, page 80).

Finishing

1. Your *Tiny Trees* quilt top is complete. Layer the quilt top, batting, and backing; baste and quilt as desired; and bind (page 53). Add a sleeve and a label to your quilt.

2. Hand stitch 24 buttons to hold the prairie points in place.

Facing the Sun

Finished quilt size: 20″ × 28½″

Facing the Sun by Patricia Drennan, 2005

Simply charming! There's no other way to describe this whimsical sunflower design with butterflies swirling around it. Pat combined foundation-pieced geese in the leaves of the sunflower, along with circular rows of couched yarns to create the center of the flower. The flower and butterflies form a large circle that, along with the leaves and stem, is appliquéd onto a sky fabric background. Here, the design drawing and subsequent instructions are slightly simplified from the project photo for ease of construction.

This little quilt was the result of a drafting session with Gail Garber. It wasn't long before I began seeing butterflies in the sky surrounding a large sunflower with flying geese leaves. The name of the piece followed naturally due to the more conspicuous movement of this flower as it reacts to the sun. —*Patricia*

Design

Materials

Blue batik background and upper binding: 1½ yards

Print sunflower center circle: 7″ × 7″ square

Yellow sunflower points: ¼ yard

Green tiny diamonds: ⅛ yard

Pink batik butterflies: ¼ yard

Dark green lower leaf section: ½ yard

Light green upper leaf section: ¼ yard

Multicolor print leaf flying geese and stem: ⅜ yard

Multicolor wavy lower border and lower binding: ¼ yard

Striped lower border: ⅛ yard

Backing: ⅞ yard

Batting: 22″ × 31″

Sleeve: ⅜ yard

Black embroidery floss: 1 skein

Decorative yarn: 4 yards

Cutting

Strips are cut cross-grain (selvage to selvage). A 40″ width of fabric is assumed. Template and foundation patterns A and G are on pattern pullout page P1.

Blue batik background:
First, before you cut anything else:

Cut 1 rectangle 25½″ × 20″ and set it aside for the background.

Cut 1 strip 4″ wide. Subcut into 9 squares 4″ × 4″. Cut these in half diagonally to make 18 triangles for the butterfly ring.

Cut 2 strips 3¼″ wide. Subcut into 18 squares 3¼″ × 3¼″ for the butterfly ring.

Cut 1 strip 2″ wide. Subcut into 12 squares 2″ × 2″. Cut these in half diagonally to make 24 triangles for the tiny background pieces next to the green diamonds in the sunflower ring.

Cut 1 strip 4″ wide. Subcut into 12 rectangles 2½″ × 4″ for the inside sunflower ring.

Cut 1 strip 4½″ wide. Subcut into 6 pieces using template pattern E for the bottom wedges of the butterfly rings.

Cut 3 strips 2¼″ wide for binding.

Print sunflower center circle:
Cut 1 using template pattern A.

Yellow sunflower points:
Cut 3 strips 2″ wide. Subcut into 24 rectangles 3¾″ × 2″.

Green tiny diamonds:
Cut 1 strip 2″ wide. Subcut into 12 squares 2″ × 2″.

Pink batik butterflies:
Cut 1 strip 4″ wide. Subcut into 9 squares 4″ × 4″. Cut in half diagonally to make 18 triangles.

Dark green lower leaf section:
Cut 2 strips 4″ wide. Subcut into 12 squares 4″ × 4″. Cut in half diagonally to make 24 triangles.

Cut 2 strips 3″ wide. Subcut into 16 squares 3″ × 3″. Cut in half diagonally to make 32 triangles.

Light green upper leaf section:
Cut 1 strip 3″ wide. Subcut into 12 squares 3″ × 3″. Cut in half diagonally to make 24 triangles.

Cut 2 strips 2″ wide. Subcut into 14 squares 2″ × 2″. Cut in half diagonally to make 28 triangles.

Multicolor print leaf flying geese and stem:
Cut 5 strips 2″ wide. Subcut as needed (shown on foundation section F on pattern pullout page P1) to make 56 geese.

Cut 1 strip 1″ × 13″ for the stem.

Multicolor wavy lower border and lower binding:
Place template pattern G on folded fabric and cut 1 piece including seam allowances. It will measure approximately 20″ × 1¾″ unfolded.

Cut 1 strip 2¼″ wide for binding.

Striped lower border:
Cut 1 strip 20″ × 3″, making sure that the stripe is vertical.

Sleeve:
Cut 1 strip 20″ × 8½″.

Foundations

Using the method described in Making Multiple Foundations of the Same Piece (page 47), make freezer-paper foundations for the following pieces:

B: Make 12.

C: Make 9.

D: Make 9.

F: Make 2 and 2 mirror images.

Construction

SUNFLOWER AND BUTTERFLIES

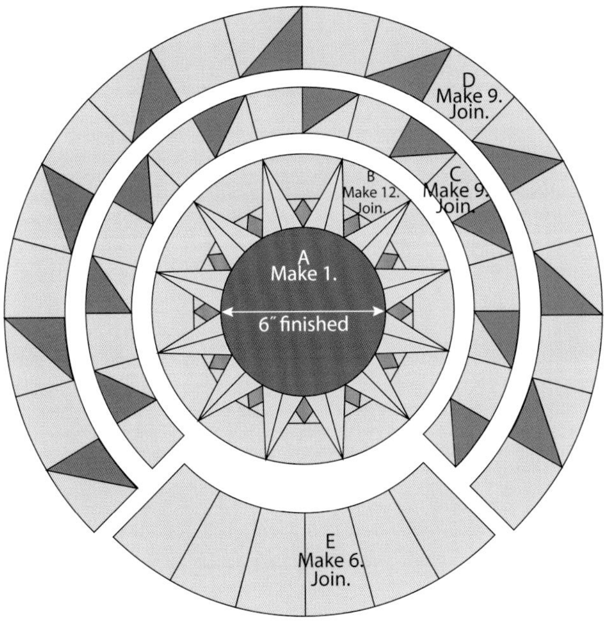

Sunflower Assembly Diagram. Sunflower circle measures 17½″ finished.

Foundation B

1. Following the method described in Stitching the Strips (pages 49–52), paper piece the B foundations. Trim the outside seam allowances to ¼″.

2. Stitch 12 B foundations together to form a circular border. Remove the paper. Press.

3. Using your favorite method, appliqué the center A to the inside edge of this circular border to form unit A/B.

Foundations C and D

1. Following the method described in Stitching the Strips (pages 49–52), paper piece the C and D foundations. Trim the outside seam allowances to ¼″.

2. Stitch the C pieces together to form an arc. Press. Remove the paper.

3. Repeat Step 2 with the D pieces. You will have 2 separate arcs.

4. Stitch these 2 arcs together with the C pieces on the inner side to make the outer C/D arc. Press.

Template Pattern E

1. Stitch the 6 E pieces together to form the lower part of the outer circular border. Press.

2. Stitch the unit from Step 1 to the outer C/D arc on both ends to complete the outer circular border. Press.

3. Using your favorite method of appliqué, stitch this completed outer circular border to the inner sunflower unit A/B.

4. Using a stem stitch, embroider the butterfly antennae with black embroidery floss.

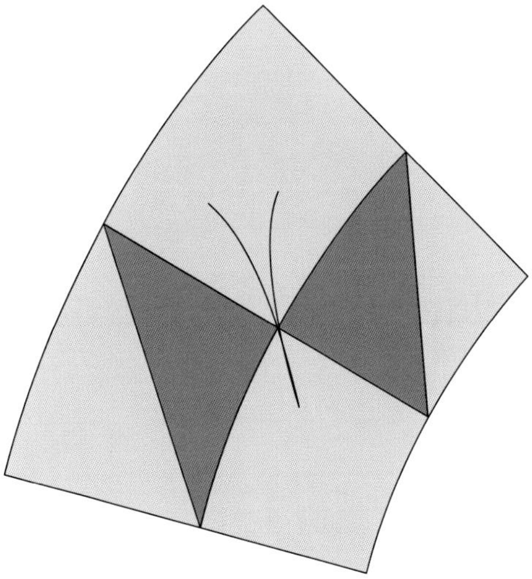

Butterfly antennae embroidery

LEAVES

Foundation F

Following the method described in Stitching the Strips (pages 49–52), paper piece 2 F foundations and 2 mirror-image F foundations. Trim the outside seam allowances to ¼″. Press. Remove the paper. Position the leaves on the background so their inner raw edges will be covered by the stem of the sunflower.

ASSEMBLY

1. Using your favorite method, appliqué the sunflower and butterfly circle, the leaves, the stem, and the wavy lower border (G) in place as shown in the Assembly Diagram (below). Cut away the background fabric behind the appliqués. (Note that the leaves and stem are slightly simplified from the project photo.)

2. Add the striped bottom border.

Assembly Diagram

Finishing

1. Your quilt top is complete. Layer the quilt top, batting, and backing; baste and quilt as desired.

2. Use a zigzag stitch and neutral thread to couch the yarns in place over the center of the sunflower.

TWO-FABRIC BINDING

Pat created a two-color binding for *Facing the Sun* with blue batik next to the sky and a different color for the lower portion. The binding for the lower portion is the same as the fabric used in the wavy lower border. For simplicity, the binding was applied using squared corners and stitched to the back in these project instructions.

1. For the top and bottom binding, cut 1 strip each of blue and multicolor that measures 2¼″ × 21″. Fold the strips in half lengthwise and press.

2. For the side binding pieces, cut 2 strips of multicolor that measure 2¼″ × 7″. Cut 2 strips of blue fabric that measure 2¼″ × 28″. Stitch a blue and a multicolor side strip together with a diagonal seam. Press the seam open. Fold the strips in half lengthwise and press. Repeat with the other pair, angling the diagonal seam the opposite way.

3. Line up the raw edges of the side bindings with the raw edges of the quilt sides. Refer to the quilt photo (page 67) and position the side bindings on the front of the quilt so the intersections between the lower border and blue sky fabric are aligned with the change in colors in the quilt.

4. Stitch the side binding strips in place. Turn the folded edge of the binding to the back of the quilt and stitch in place. Trim the binding ends even with the corners of the quilt.

5. Measure the width of the top and bottom of the quilt including the side bindings. Trim the top and bottom binding strips to this length plus 1″. Align the long raw edges of the binding with the quilt top and bottom, leaving ½″ at each end of the binding extending past the quilt. Stitch. Fold over the ends of the binding before turning to the back of the quilt so they finish even with the sides of the quilt. Stitch the bindings in place on the back of the quilt.

6. After binding, add a sleeve and a label to your quilt.

Rueda de la Fortuna
(Wheel of Fortune)

Finished quilt size: 37½″ × 38½″

Block size: 18½″ × 19″ finished

Rueda de la Fortuna by Gail Garber and Donna Barnitz, 2008

Life is not constant. It ebbs and flows like a pendulum over the course of our lives; some years are more memorable than others. ***Rueda,*** *or "wheel," embodies the fluidity that has shaped who I have become. Overall, the brilliant colors reflect my wonder of the world that surrounds me, and the quilt highlights the most positive aspects of my life. I hope that you also find inspiration in your "wheel of fortune."*

Design

Rueda is a block repeat design. One block is mirrored, and then this pair is also mirrored to make four blocks. Note that the design drawing is slightly simplified from the project photo for ease of construction.

Materials

This list shows the colors I used. Some of the yardage requirements might appear to be overly generous, particularly for the turquoise and the multicolor warms. I elected to use 2 pieces of hand-painted Skydyes fabrics (Resources, page 79) for these. Both were directional fabrics and required additional yardage in order to accommodate the positioning of the 2 large rings. The yardage below is figured for directional fabric for the 3 sections of the rings (C, E, and F, shown on page 74).

Additionally, yardage requirements are generous for ease of placement of the long tips and sharp angles.

Turquoise center star: ½ yard

Yellow center star background: ⅝ yard

Orange center star background: ½ yard

Multicolor warms inner ring: ½ yard

Red sunrays inner border: 1¼ yards

Yellow to purple sunrays inner border background: 1¼ yards

Blue hand-painted outer ring and 4 small diamonds: 1 yard

Peach outer border geese: 1 yard

Purple scraps outer border background: 1⅜ yards

Backing: 1¼ yards

Batting: 41" × 47"

Binding (cut on the bias): ½ yard

Cutting

Strips are cut cross-grain (selvage to selvage). A 40″ width of fabric is assumed. Use the template patterns and foundations on the pullouts (pattern pullout page P2).

Turquoise center star:
Cut 2 strips 6½″ wide. Subcut these into 32 rectangles 2¼″ × 6½″.

Yellow center star background:
Cut 3 strips 5½″ wide. Subcut these into 16 squares 5½″ × 5½″.

Orange center star background:
Cut 2 strips 5½″ wide. Subcut these into 16 rectangles 4½″ × 5½″.

Multicolor warms inner ring:
Cut 2 plus 2 mirror-image pieces using the section C template pattern. For this section it might be preferable to divide this large piece in half for easier piecing. Remember to add a central seam allowance if you choose this option. Align the straight of grain of the fabric with the lines drawn on the pattern. Transfer registration marks to the wrong side of the fabric.

Red sunrays inner border:
Cut 6 strips 6″ wide. Subcut these into 68 rectangles 3″ × 6″.

Yellow to purple sunrays inner border background:
Cut 7 strips 6″ wide. Subcut these into 68 rectangles 3¾″ × 6″.

Blue hand-painted outer ring and diamonds:
Cut 2 plus 2 mirror-image pieces using the sections E and F template patterns. Align the straight of grain of the fabric with the lines drawn on the patterns. Transfer registration marks to the wrong side of the fabric.

Cut 4 rectangles 1½″ × 3″ for the side diamonds in section G.

Cut 4 rectangles 2″ × 3″ for the top and bottom diamonds in section I.

Peach outer border geese:
Large geese: Cut 2 strips 3″ wide. Subcut these into 12 rectangles 6″ × 3″.

Small geese: Cut 6 strips 4″ wide. Subcut these into 72 rectangles 3″ × 4″.

Purple scraps outer border background:
Larger geese backgrounds: Cut 4 strips 5″ wide. Subcut these into 30 squares 5″ × 5″. Cut in half diagonally. For piece 35 in foundation G, cut 4 rectangles 4½″ × 3″.

Small geese backgrounds: Cut 5 strips 3½″ wide. Subcut these into 54 squares 3½ × 3½″. Cut in half diagonally.

Binding:
Cut enough strips of 2¼″-wide bias binding to make 1 long strip about 180″ long.

Foundations

Using the method described in Making Multiple Foundations of the Same Piece (page 47), make 4 freezer-paper foundations (2 of which will be mirror images) for the following pieces: A, B, D, G, H, and I.

Construction

1. Following the method described in Stitching the Strips (pages 49–52), paper piece all the foundation sections (A, B, D, G, H, and I).

Once all the sections are complete, trim the seam allowances to ¼″. Transfer the registration marks to the wrong side of the fabric before removing the paper. When stitching curved seams, the paper must be removed before stitching.

2. Stitch section A to section B to create the center star. Press the seams toward the side of least resistance.

3. Carefully match and pin all registration marks between the center star A/B and the inner ring (section C). (It also might be necessary to pin between registration marks.) Stitch unit A/B to section C. Press.

4. Matching registration marks and pinning carefully, stitch unit A/B/C to section D. Press.

5. Stitch sections E and F together and press. Matching registration marks and pinning carefully, add this unit to the already stitched sections. Press.

6. Stitch sections G, H, and I together. Press. Matching registration marks and pinning carefully, add it to the already stitched sections as the final outer border. Press.

7. Repeat Steps 2–6 to make 3 more blocks. Remember that 2 are mirror images of the original block.

8. Using the quilt photograph (page 71) as your model, place the 4 blocks so the center stars emerge. Stitch the 2 top blocks together. Press. Repeat with the remaining 2 blocks.

9. Stitch the 2 pairs from Step 8 together. Press.

10. Join the bias binding strips together to make 1 strip approximately 180″ long.

Block Assembly Diagram

Finishing

Your quilt top is complete. Layer the quilt top, batting, and backing; baste and quilt as desired; and bind (page 53). Add a sleeve and a label to your quilt.

Anova I by Gail Garber, 20″ × 20″. In the collection of Patricia Drennan.

This small quilt is made of only one block.

Winding Ways

Finished quilt size: 70½″ × 70½″

Block size: 12″ × 12″ finished

Winding Ways by Gail Garber, Michele Hymel, and Donna Barnitz, 2008

What a great quilt! This take on the old-fashioned block-style quilt is anything but vintage. We've designed the Winding Ways block to include lots of geese. The gradations weave in and out to create a complex pattern that is simply stunning. Starting with a twenty-step fabric gradation pack from Starr Design Fabrics Starr Fire (Resources, page 79), the geese move through the colors of the rainbow.

The gradations used here include yellow, yellow-orange, orange, red-orange, red, red-fuchsia, fuchsia, violet, yellow-green, lime, light green, green, blue-green, blue, purple, and dark fuchsia.

I used four different colorations in the foundation-pieced blocks in this quilt, as shown below. I also used a gradation fabric for the block backgrounds, with the darkest fabric in the outermost blocks gradating to the lightest fabric in the innermost blocks to give this quilt a little extra pizzazz!

Hand-dyed gradation pack

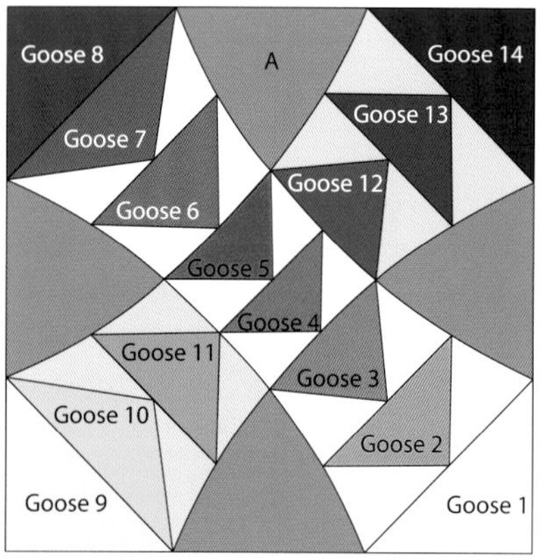

Block A design color arrangement

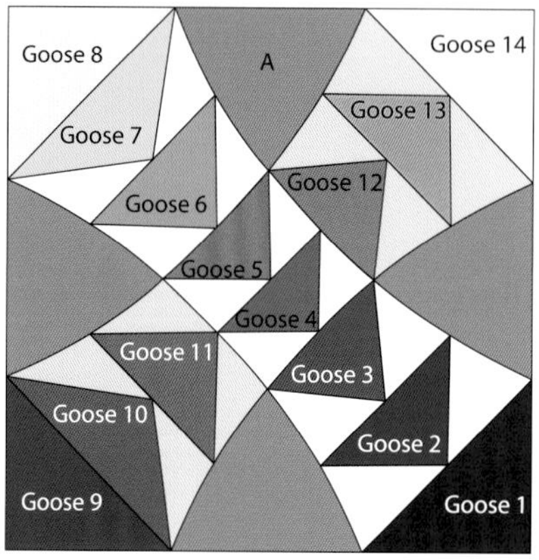

Block B design color arrangement

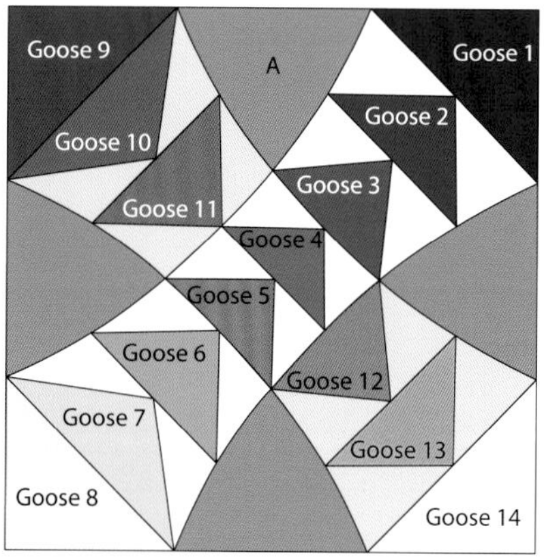

Block C design color arrangement

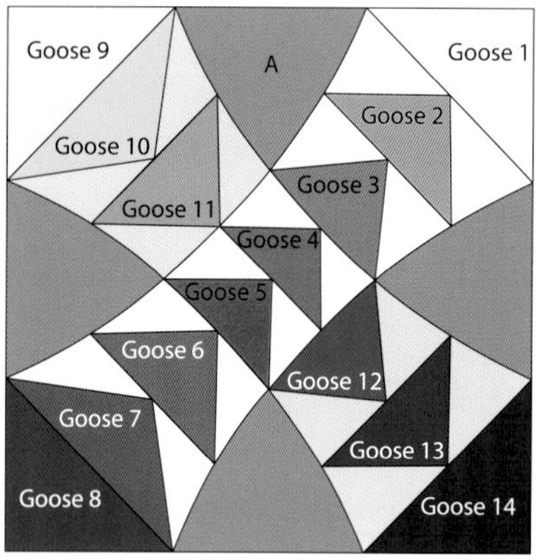

Block D design color arrangement

Noto

Enlarge and photocopy the design illustration to the right to color and experiment with different color arrangements.

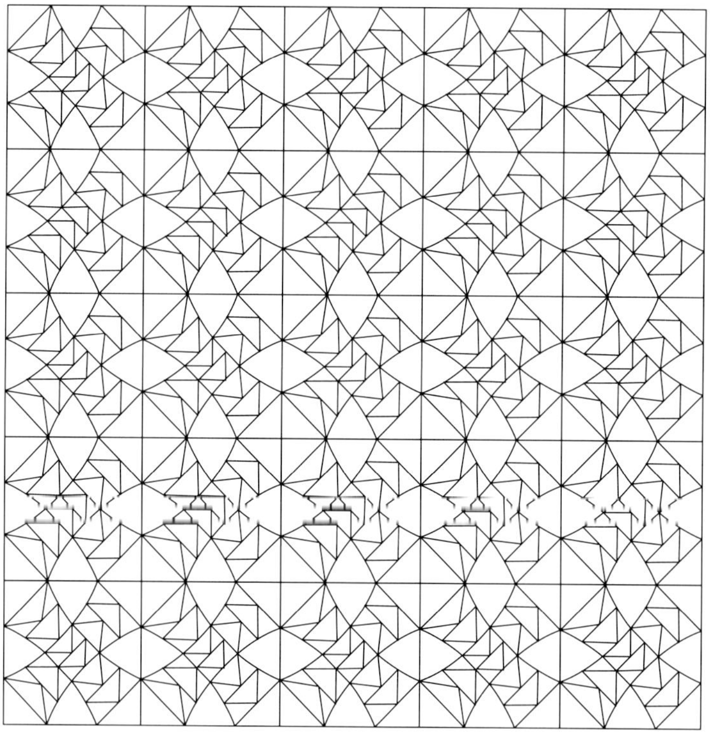

Design

Materials

Note

This quilt can be made using a fat-quarter pack of 16-step gradations, but there is no extra fabric in some colors for errors. I recommend purchasing a ½-yard pack; you will have leftovers.

Gradations geese: ½-yard pack of 16-step gradations or the equivalent in color-graded batiks

Light blue background (over units): 2⅜ yards

Medium blue background (under units): 2 yards

Multicolor gradation fabric block filler background: 1½ yards

Multicolor hand-dyed border: 1⅜ yards

Backing: 4¼ yards

Binding: ⅝ yard

Batting: 75″ × 75″

Sleeve: ⅝ yard

Cutting

Strips are cut cross-grain (selvage to selvage). A 40″ width of fabric is assumed. The templates and foundation patterns for this project are on pullout page P1. Cut pieces are sized with little extra in the seam allowances to best utilize the gradation packs.

Gradations: *yellow, yellow-orange, fuchsia, violet, purple, yellow-green, lime, and dark fuchsia geese*
From each color, cut 6 squares 7¼″ × 7¼″. Cut diagonally in both directions to make 24 triangles. Use 1 triangle as a template to cut a 25th triangle from leftover fabric.

Gradations: *orange, red-fuchsia, light green, and blue geese*
From each color, cut 6 squares 6″ × 6″. Cut diagonally in both directions to make 24 triangles. Use 1 triangle as a template to cut a 25th triangle from leftover fabric.

Gradations: *green, blue-green, red-orange, and red geese*
From each color, cut 3 squares 6″ × 6″. Cut diagonally in both directions to make 12 triangles. Use 1 triangle as a template to cut a 13th triangle from leftover fabric of the red or red-orange pieces.

Light blue background:
For geese 3–6: Cut 10 strips 4″ wide. Subcut each strip into 10 squares 4″ × 4″. Cut each square once diagonally to make 200 triangles.

For geese 2 and 7: Cut 7 strips 5″ wide. Subcut each strip into 8 squares 5″ × 5″. Cut each square diagonally to make 100 triangles (you will have extra).

Medium blue background:
For geese 10–13: Cut 13 strips 5″ wide. Subcut each strip into 8 squares 5″ × 5″. Cut each square diagonally to make 200 triangles (you will have extra).

Multicolor gradation fabric block filler background:
Cut 10 strips 4½″ wide. Use template pattern A (pattern pullout page P1) to cut 11 units from each strip by alternating the direction that the point faces as shown. Cut 100 total of template pattern A.

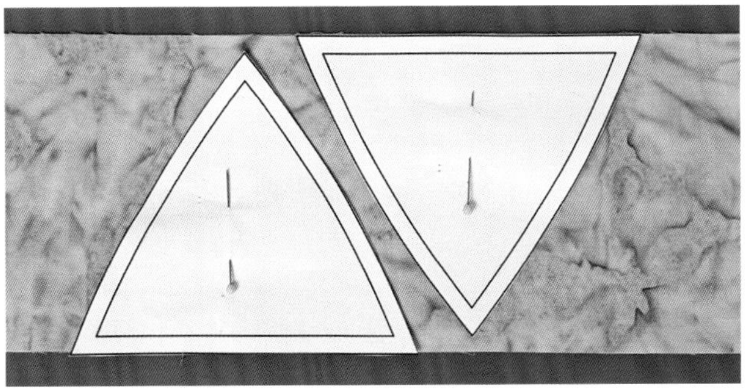

Cut template pattern A.

Note

For the block filler background, use the darkest fabric in the outermost blocks, gradating to the lightest fabric in the innermost blocks.

Multicolor hand-dyed border:
Cut 8 strips 5½″ wide.

Binding:
Cut 8 strips 2¼″ wide.

Sleeve:
Cut 2 strips 8½″ wide. Trim to 35½″ long.

Foundations and Templates

Using the method described in Making Multiple Foundations of the Same Piece (page 47), make 25 freezer-paper foundations each for pieces B, C, and D (pattern pullout page P1).

Construction

1. Following the method described in Freezer-Paper Foundation Piecing (pages 44–53), paper piece foundations B, C, and D, following the stitching order on the foundation patterns.

Make 9 of the block A color arrangement. Make 6 each of the blocks B and C color arrangements. Make 4 of the block D color arrangement. Be sure to label your blocks. Press. Remove paper.

2. Assemble the blocks using the color arrangements above with the foundation placement shown below.

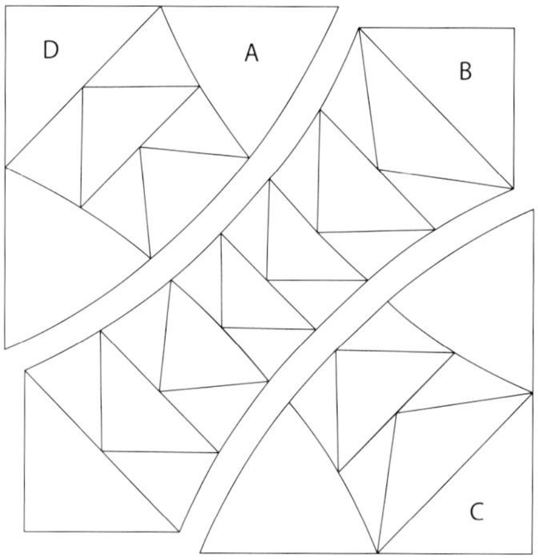

Block assembly for blocks A and B (matches front view of finished quilt)

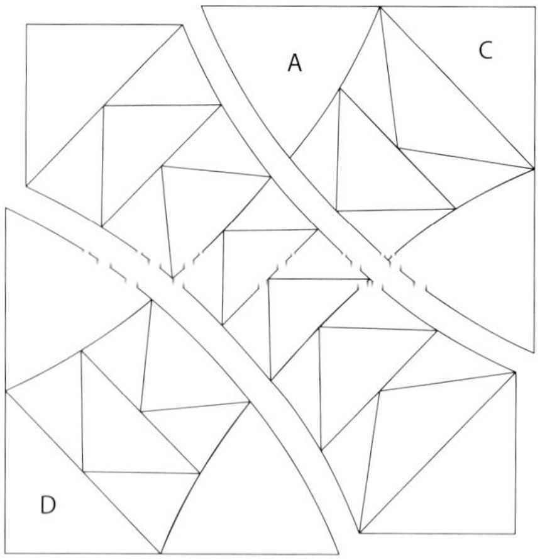

Block assembly for blocks C and D (matches front view of finished quilt)

3. Refer to the Quilt Assembly Diagram (below) to stitch the blocks together in rows. Press.

Note

Lay out the quilt blocks as shown in the illustration, or go your own way and develop your own design. The choice is yours!

4. Stitch the rows together. Press.

Quilt Assembly Diagram

OUTER BORDER

1. Stitch 2 border strips together to make a strip 80″ × 5½″. Press. Repeat to make 3 more.

2. Center each border piece over the quilt top. Pin in place. With your sewing machine needle ½″ from the quilt top corner, backstitch to ¼″ from the edge of the quilt, and then stitch forward until reaching the end of the quilt top. Backstitch. Repeat on the remaining sides.

Fold the edges and miter the corners (page 63).

Finishing

Your quilt top is complete. Layer the quilt top, batting, and backing; baste and quilt as desired; and bind (page 53). Add a sleeve and a label to your quilt.

Photo by Richard Kilme

About the Author

A quiltmaker for over 30 years, Gail came to this craft innocently enough when her friends talked her into taking the beginning quilting class that was to change her life. A dabbler by nature, Gail tried her hand at several different techniques.

It was only a matter of time before Gail, who has a background in math, began exploring original design with emphasis on geometric shapes. It was here that she met the unrepentant wayward goose, initially corralling it into circles that were inspired by fellow artists Jinny Beyer and Judy Mathieson. But the goose had other ideas. Following a brainstorming session with the goose, the irreverent duo diverged from tradition into an exhilarating world filled with exploration and new shapes.

Her award-winning work has been exhibited in many national quilt shows and published in numerous magazines. She teaches and lectures worldwide, and particularly enjoys traveling and meeting new friends wherever she goes.

In her other life, Gail is the founder and executive director of Hawks Aloft, Inc., a nonprofit conservation organization founded in 1994 that is based in Albuquerque, New Mexico. The organization works to conserve indigenous wild birds through avian research, education, and cooperation with others. One of the key components of Hawks Aloft is its statewide conservation education program that features nonreleasable birds of prey. Several of these educational ambassadors reside on the Garber property, where they live in large flight cages suited to their various injuries. These, along with two rescued Cairn Terriers, comprise the Garber menagerie that guarantees there never will be a dull moment. *Gail's website:* www.gailgarberdesigns.com

Resources

C&T Publishing
Rulers, freezer paper
800-284-1114
www.ctpub.com

Carol Doak
Paper-piecing teacher, books, supplies
www.caroldoak.com

Cedar Canyon Textiles
Shiva Artist's Paintstiks
877-296-9278
www.cedarcanyontextiles.com

Cherrywood Fabrics
Hand-dyed fabrics
888-298-0967
www.cherrywoodfabrics.com

Fons and Porter
Mechanical fabric pencils
866-729-9601
www.fonsandporter.com

Frieda Anderson
Hand-dyed fabrics
847-697-6557
www.friestyle.com

Gail Garber Designs
Drawing tools, flexible curves, compasses, rulers
505-892-3354
www.gailgarberdesigns.com

Little Foot
That Purple Thang (loosens paper from small areas)
800-597-7075
www.littlefoot.net

Skydyes
Hand-dyed, hand-painted fabrics
www.skydyes.com

Starr Design Fabrics, Inc.
Gradated color packs
530-467-5121
www.starrfabrics.com

For a list of other fine books from C&T Publishing, ask for a free catalog:

C&T PUBLISHING, INC.
P.O. Box 1456
Lafayette, CA 94549
800-284-1114
Email: ctinfo@ctpub.com
Website: www.ctpub.com

C&T Publishing's professional photography services are now available to the public. Visit us at www.ctmediaservices.com.

Tips and Techniques *can be found at www.ctpub.com > Consumer Resources > Quiltmaking Basics: Tips & Techniques for Quiltmaking & More*

For quilting supplies:

COTTON PATCH
1025 Brown Ave.
Lafayette, CA 94549
Store: 925-284-1177
Mail order: 925-283-7883
Email: CottonPa@aol.com
Website: www.quiltusa.com

Note: Fabrics used in the quilts shown may not be currently available, as fabric manufacturers keep most fabrics in print for only a short time.